D0646969

CANADA FROM THE AIR

Bo Curtis & J. A. Kraulis

Hurtig Publishers

Edmonton

Hurtig Publishers Ltd.
10560 — 105 Street
Edmonton, Alberta

Canadian Cataloguing in Publication Data

Curtis, Bo, 1950-
    Canada from the air

    ISBN 0-888-30-201-0

    1. Canada — Description and travel — 1950-*
I. Kraulis, J. A., 1949-   II. Title.

FC75.C87   917.1'04644   C81-091189-2
F1016.C87

Printed and bound in Canada

Page one: An autumn-gold patch of aspen, the most widely distributed
tree species on the continent, carpets the Porcupine Hills, prelude to
the Rockies in southern Alberta.

Page two: According to climate data, the Okanagan Valley in British
Columbia has the longest summer in Canada. Just off the sidewalk in
Penticton crowds take advantage of the warm water of Skaha Lake.

Above: Low in elevation and gentle in slope, the treeless Richardson
Mountains in northern Yukon support vegetation only in their valleys
and on the most sheltered slopes.

For my parents
Bo Curtis

In memory of dear friends
Uldis Auders and Raymond Jotterand
J. A. Kraulis

Above: Despite their comparatively modest altitude, the few
mountains that constitute the Spectrum Range in Mount Edziza Park
are among the most conspicuous in British Columbia, vividly coloured
by iron oxides present in light-coloured volcanic rocks.

Pages 8/9: This circular feedlot in Lethbridge, Alberta, is designed for
maximum efficiency in the handling of animals. The wedge-shaped
pens permit easy herding of the cattle, which are fed along the outside
perimeters from the stockpiled hay visible as light-coloured clusters
resembling so many bread loaves.

Preface

This book is the product of numerous flights, including four coast-to-coast trips, made over a two-year period. The "flight across Canada" described in the text is actually a composite of these flights, and as such did not take place exactly as described. It is, however, a typical trip across the country by light aircraft, and we did experience, at one time or another, each sensation, sight, or event.

Our first flights were made in rented aircraft, but it quickly became apparent that in order to have the degree of freedom we needed, we would have to buy or lease one of our own. At this point, a real friend appeared in Colin Jackson. His sweet little Piper Pacer filled the bill nicely, and with a bit of persuasion we horn-swaggled him into relinquishing it to us. But it was not the last he saw of it; at times when we were unable to look after it properly, he cared for it, flew it, nursed it through mechanical ailments, and even pinch-hit as pilot for a trip. Our debt to him is immeasurable.

One of the greatest obstacles in the production of this book has been the fact that the authors usually live at opposite ends of the country. While Janis is constantly on the go with various photographic projects and is difficult to reach, my job as lightkeeper has kept me on an isolated island, with erratic mail and no phone, and hence equally difficult to contact. Most of our correspondence has been by cassette tape. Once, after a month without mail, I received no less than ten cassettes at the same time: fourteen hours of rather dry, one-sided conversation! But by far the biggest problem in keeping a lighthouse and simultaneously trying to produce a book is in finding the time off, and in this respect the effort and support of Allan and Darlene Tansky and W. M. Exley of the Canadian Coast Guard have been of immense help.

For some reason private aviation has gained a reputation as a rich man's hobby, and when you fly your own plane, people expect you to go in style, your pockets bulging with extra cash. But when a near-antique aircraft arrives on the field, bearing blue-jeaned occupants who pitch tents under the wing, the image of penny-pinching aviators is more credible. We could easily have doubled our expenses and our problems were it not for the hospitality of Dr. and Mrs. Maurice Young, Dave Malcolm and Megan Whittingham, Pat Mazier, Arvo and Debbi Koppel, Judy Currelly and Doug LeMond, Phil and Claudette Upton, Graham and Alex Young, Pat Morrow, Ron and Judith Henry, Anthony Whittingham, Tony Perzel, Tom and Andrea Duchastel, Jack Scott and Sue Wyard, Rob Curtis and Barbara Holmes, Rita and Dzidris Silins, Boo and Rafe Currrelly, David Hadden, and Janis's parents. They all made our travels a pleasure.

Further assistance has been given by Andris Rudzitis, Douglas Lowe, Paul Davison, Chris Schlachter, Jean-Paul Duquette, Damian Regan, Gilles Lepage, David Shaw and José Druker. The assistance of the many air traffic controllers, radio operators, and weather briefers across Canada has made this project easier, and their cheerful, competent services were depended upon constantly. The skilled hands of Ray Williams, Doug Scott, and Barney Oldfield were responsible for keeping our airplane in top condition, and the trust we placed in their abilities when high over Cabot Strait or the mountains of the Yukon proved to be well-founded.

The persistent use of imperial measures in this book may raise some eyebrows at the Metric Commission, but *thousands of feet* and *miles* are universally used in aviation, and to use metric equivalents would be artificial. Then, too, the land was originally measured in imperial units, and the proportions and dimensions of the imperial system are everywhere manifest in farmland, town plans, buildings. To use metric measures would appear inappropriate.

In the beside-every-man-is-a-great-woman department, my wife, Cathy, has quite literally been beside me at every stage of the book's progress. She has served enthusiastically as navigator, co-pilot, gas jockey, editor, mentor, and general right-hand lady throughout, and the true degree to which my share of this book is hers as well as mine will be my closely-guarded secret, lest I be accused of taking credit that is not my due.

A no less substantial role was played by Linda, Janis's guardian of peace and sanity, during his struggle with some fourteen thousand colour transparencies and a library of contradictory and elusive information.

And finally we would like to thank Mel Hurtig, whose role as publisher has, in our eyes, been secondary in importance to the kind encouragement, guidance, and support he has given us since the beginning.

Bo Curtis

Introduction

In an age when rapid transcontinental travel is not only possible, but considered practical and routine, it would seem likely that a growing appreciation for the diversity of the country's landscape would be a natural by-product of modern aviation. But ironically enough, the very efficiency and reliability of air transportation has made flight an almost mundane means of travel. Complete with hot meals and in-flight entertainment, the airliner has long outgrown the days when men strove to put themselves in the air for one reason only: to witness the spectacle of their world from above.

But airliners are as different from our little single-engined plane as an ocean liner is from a canoe. A light plane can't compete with an airliner in crossing the country in comfort and on schedule. If the intention is to observe what is below, however, then the light airplane excels.

It was indeed our intention to observe Canada from the air, to feast on her celebrated beauty from a perspective not widely experienced or documented. The airplane we used was small, noisy, cramped, and slow, but it was also uncomplicated and docile, allowing us to focus our attention outside the windows. Given time and good weather, it carried us faithfully from British Columbia to Newfoundland, from the Mackenzie Delta to Labrador, and at one time touched down in all ten provinces in seven days of flying. We went to these places for no reason other than to see and photograph them, and to learn more about the country through one of the most evocative and entertaining means possible — flight.

As can be expected, we learned much about the geography of Canada, of its coastlines and mountains, of the rivers and lakes, the cities and towns. From the air the country is, after all, laid out like a map, and veteran airline travellers may find nothing remarkable about seeing the land spread out below them. But we have seen a great deal that is missed from 35,000 feet; we have seen the character of the nation and its people. We have peered into city streets and backyards, seen Canadians at work and at play, on farm fields and on fishing dories, on golf courses and on beaches. We have watched freight trains churning through mountain passes, ore carriers negotiating seaway locks, and grain ships loading cargoes for the Orient.

We have closely studied the land itself in a way that airliners will never allow; rolling surf on a log-strewn beach, boiling waters spilling down a remote northern stream, awesome glaciers, magnificent waterfalls, mysterious swamps. We have seen how man has shaped the landscape so that each part of the country bears his own cultural signature: the abstract art of the prairie farm, the calligraphy of the urban highway, the repetition of suburbia, the profanity of industrial waste, the austerity of a seaport town, the tranquility of a mountain homestead. The airplane is capable not only of bringing these scenes to our attention, but of putting them into perspective, of knitting them into a composite, living portrait of the country.

And the experience of light plane travel is more than a visual one. The small aircraft is at one with the atmosphere, with the wind and weather that are in turn very much a part of the country over which the plane travels. It will tumble in the turbulence of a mountain pass, ride a chinook across the shortgrass prairie, soar in the thermals of a midsummer afternoon, or grope through the mists of a Cape Breton morning.

A country the size and richness of Canada presents an infinity of images to the keen aerial observer. The text and photographs that follow offer but a fraction of this experience, a sampling of the joys, puzzles, and insights awaiting the air traveller. For those fortunate enough to have flown in a light plane over Canada, or parts of Canada, we hope this book will recreate their experiences for them. For those who have not yet seen Canada from above, we offer this book as a modest substitute until they have the opportunity to do so. And for those airline passengers who have flown over Canada, but without seeing it, we trust this book will tempt them away from the movies to gaze out the windows.

Above: The official residence of the prime minister since 1951, 24 Sussex Drive is a grey stone mansion overlooking the Ottawa River.

Opposite: One of two official residences of the Governor General of Canada (the other is the Citadel in Quebec), Rideau Hall, or Government House, is far more palatial than the nearby 24 Sussex. Here the Governor General, who officially outranks the prime minister, hosts visiting heads of state.

Opposite: "We invite you to stop and share the beauty that is around us," welcomes a sincere roadside sign at one of the towns on Nova Scotia's Atlantic coast. In an airplane one cannot stop; but from above, the beauty is apparent everywhere. This is Rose Bay, a small fishing settlement of a few hundred people.

Above: Fishermen's sheds and colourfully painted dories line the shore of Bottle Cove, a perfect little harbour tucked in behind the sea cliffs that barricade much of the western shore of Newfoundland. Despite government encouragement of centralized big-boat fishing fleets, many islanders still earn their livelihoods in such remote and independent outports.

Above: With its graceful concrete arches, the pool in Nathan Phillips Square provides a complementary foreground for Toronto City Hall. The wind direction (frequently important information to pilots) is readily apparent from the wet pavement on the lee side of the fountain. In winter, the pool becomes a popular skating rink.

Opposite: Designed by Viljo Revell, a Finnish architect who won an international competition for the project, Toronto City Hall expresses the functions of city government. The domed council chamber nestles between two soaring municipal office towers, a 20-storey one visible as the arc at the bottom of the picture, and a 27-storey one curving out of the picture to the left.

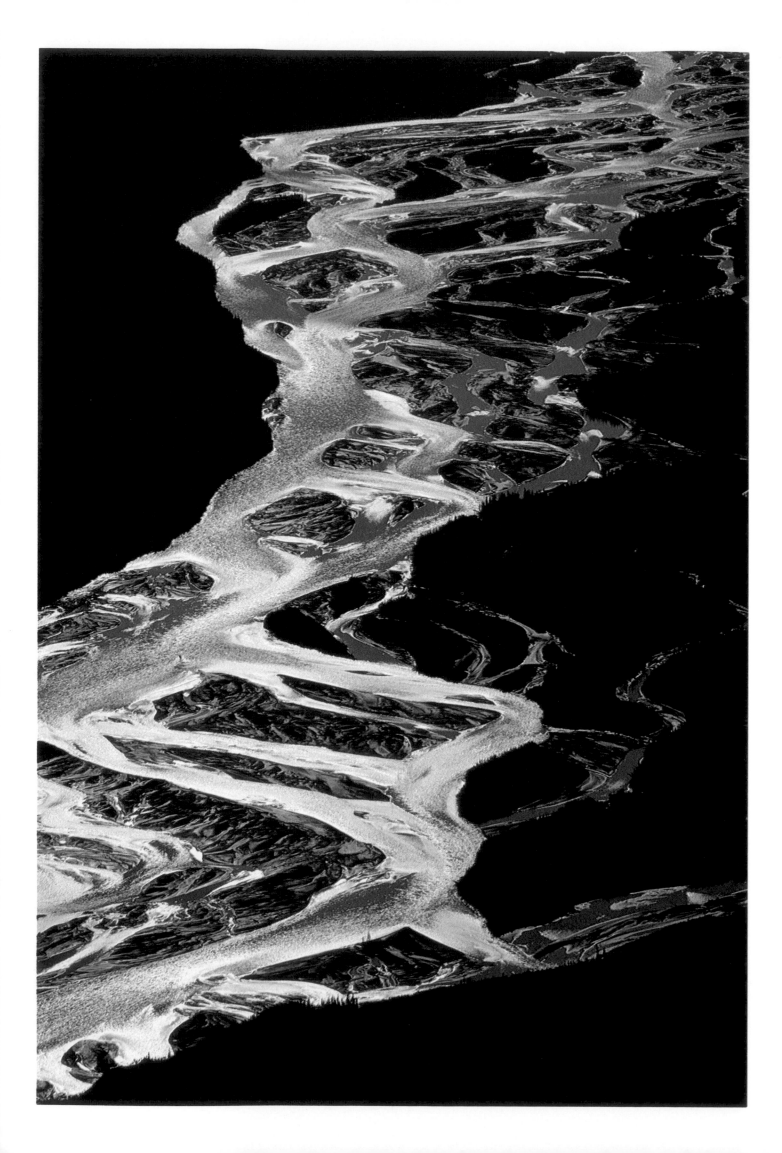

Opposite: Tributary of the Yukon River, the White River carries the melt from the icefields of the St. Elias Mountains. Constantly shifting with its heavy sediment load, exploring divergent paths of least resistance, the dense stream braids a many-channelled course down the broad flat valley floor once scoured by a massive glacier.

Above: Burying mountains up to their necks, the icefields covering the southwestern corner of the Yukon are the largest outside of Antarctica, Greenland and a few Arctic islands. Here, in this sterile white sanctuary amidst Canada's highest peaks, one can appreciate the immensity of the frozen burden which, just yesterday in geological terms, squashed virtually the entire country.

Deserted early in the morning except for a couple of thoroughbreds in training, Stampede Park in Calgary reveals the vivid colours of its unobscured grandstand seats. The scene of horse races most of the time, for ten days each July it stages "the greatest outdoor show on earth," attracting huge crowds to the exhibitions, the midway rides and, above all, the rodeo of the Calgary Stampede.

Adjacent to the CNE, the world's largest annual exhibition, Ontario
Place is built on three man-made islands off the Toronto waterfront.
Prominent in this view of the recreation centre are five suspended
pavilions containing exhibits, theatres, a restaurant and an information
centre; a marina for over three hundred boats; and the Cinesphere,
which houses one of the world's largest movie screens.

Above: Early in June, the rich red soil of Prince Edward Island is still bare, outlined by green borders of trees, shrubs, and grass. Come summer, the complementary colour scheme will be reversed. Bright green fields will be everywhere, and the red will be confined to the clay secondary roads and parking spaces.

Opposite: By mid-May, alfalfa for dairy cows is already being harvested in British Columbia's Fraser Valley, which has the longest growing season in Canada. The farmer has cut diagonally across the field to avoid crossing a shallow gully, invisible from the air, which would otherwise be too awkward for him to negotiate.

Overleaf: Much of British Columbia's timber is barged along the extensive coast and dumped at staging areas where, according to size and species, it is sorted into booms — such as these in Howe Sound north of Vancouver — and tugged away to different pulp or sawmills.

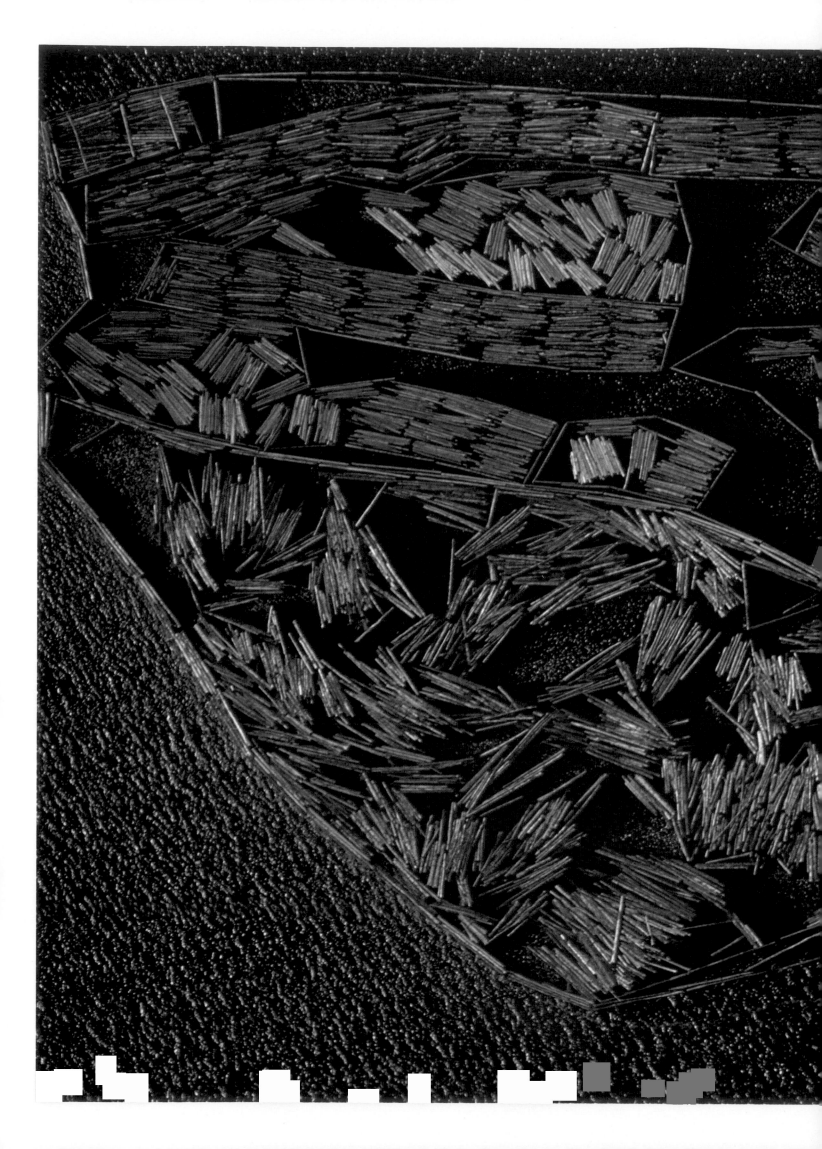

Above: As recorded in the calligraphy of moraines which stripe its melting surface, the Lowell Glacier is formed by the confluence of several dozen smaller glaciers. One of the numerous giant rivers of ice flowing from the St. Elias icefields in Kluane National Park, the glacier is more than three miles wide at the tongue and stretches forty-five miles back into the mountains.

Opposite: The rim of a basin cleared of vegetation provides a neat, clean shore for Abraham Lake on the impounded North Saskatchewan River in the Alberta Rockies. In Canada, the total area of land that has been flooded by dams exceeds the size of Holland.

Above: Preserving the path of the seeder in its flowing curves, a blooming rapeseed field contours around a stream gully near Yorkton, Saskatchewan.

Opposite: The border of a tilled field south of Edmonton retains neatly furrowed curves where a tractor-towed disker has been steered in wide circles to reverse direction. To the left, cattle graze in the fenced-off field which, occupied by sloughs and a meandering stream, is too awkward for planting. Cattle tracks are prominent on the landscape of a province where livestock outnumber humans.

Opposite: The world from the air. At the waterworks in Hamilton, Ontario, a storage tank painted as a globe has what is graphically its most effective part facing upwards. This is not to oblige airborne photographers, but rather so that the city's location on the sphere squarely faces the motorist arriving from the direction of the Burlington Skyway.

Above: Little boxes and they all look just the same, near Grand Bend on Lake Huron, Ontario. Appealing from the air and on a planner's drafting table, this type of subdivision layout provides a communal backyard play area separated from traffic. Freedom from the grid, however, is paid for with a lack of privacy resulting from the absence of defined property lines between the houses.

Overleaf: One of the oldest manned lightstations along the notched coast of British Columbia, Entrance Island guides vessels in the vicinity of Nanaimo harbour.

Every last inch of space is used, the rear seat bulging from the conglomerate of tents, sleeping bags, duffels, and toolboxes sequentially jammed into place behind it. Under the seat are boxes of film, foam sleeping pads, a rarely-used briefcase, and several cans of oil accompanied by a slimy spout-opener wrapped in plastic, a vain effort to keep it from getting oil on everything. On the seat itself a camera bag and a flurry of film wrappers surround the day's lunch (the rear seat doubles as galley, the photographer as steward). On the floor, the leg-tangling headset cord meanders under the front seat to the rat's nest of wires sprouting from the intercom, whose earphones and boom-mikes are tied into the aircraft radio. The front seat is awash in charts, logbooks, pencils, and all the bric-a-brac that goes with navigating cross-country.

The owner's manual claims a Piper Pacer will carry 800 pounds of people, fuel, and baggage, but in the twenty minutes or so it takes to find a place for it all, you get to wondering where they expect you to put it. To be fair though, she's not meant to be a freighter, and when she rolled off the assembly line in 1950, her first owners no doubt cruised up to the tarmac in their Packard or Studebaker, sank into the Pacer's plush velour seats, and proudly taxied off in the latest in personal air transportation.

And now, thirty years later, she strikes an anachronistic pose amid the turboprops at Vancouver Airport, squatting pertly on her tailwheel. Not without pride, mind you. She's a bit of a rare bird; the Pacer's numbers were limited by the success of her nosewheeled offspring, the TriPacers, which are so much more numerous that many recognize the older Pacer only as a "TriPacer with a tailwheel." But for us, the real value of her obsolete undercarriage is not rarity, but the position of the main wheels. They are forward, where they don't obstruct the view as do the main wheels of tricycle gear aircraft. Handling a taildragger on the ground can be nerve-wracking at the best of times (there *is* a reason why they are obsolete), but once we're airborne the visual joys of flight in our plane are unimpeded. Unencumbered, too, by the complexities of modern aviation; the panel is basic stuff, a few dials to keep tabs on the engine, a few more for speed and altitude, period. One very good radio, but not a single electronic gadget for navigation. For that we have maps, and eyes, and the country itself.

The Lycoming puffs into life, first time every time, a good, reliable engine. As we click through the frequencies on the radio like scanning cable TV channels, Automatic Terminal Information Service comes alive, a recorded voice giving the latest in wind, runway, and weather. ATIS is found only at major airports like Vancouver, freeing the controllers from the choking flow of numbers and allowing them to focus their attention on keeping track of us all.

"Sierra Zulu Victor, Vancouver Ground." They always invert our registration, and we always have to correct them. Neither "Z-S-V" nor the phonetically coded "Zulu Sierra Victor" seems to roll easily off the tongue, like "A-B-C" or "Alpha Bravo

Charlie." But we must live with it, for unlike automobile licence plates an aircraft's registration is its permanent identification, its name for life.

"Okay, Zulu Sierra Victor, Ground. Cleared taxi two-six."

With a modest roar we jump out of the line and waddle down the taxiway (tailwheels *are* a handful on the ground). After the runup, we switch to tower frequency and ask for takeoff clearance.

"Zulu Sierra Victor, Tower. Wait, traffic on final."

Fine, we'll wait . . . wouldn't want to tangle with this one, an L-1011 over the approach lights, landing lights blazing, undercarriage reaching for the runway like talons. Its shadow swoops over us in a black flash, the whine of its triple fan jets at idle clearly audible over the Lycoming's purr. The mammoth airliner recedes rapidly down the runway, reverse thrust thundering, a pterodactyl retreating into its cave. Inside the 1011 the public address system is by now crackling to life . . .

"Ladies and gentlemen, welcome to Vancouver. On behalf of the entire crew we would like to thank you for travelling with us . . ." Coffee cups retrieved, pillows collected, Muzak on. Legs stretching, yawns, a long routine trip from Toronto, over four hours with that headwind. The window shades come up, that sun sure was strong, and the movie was more interesting than looking out . . .

" . . . Sierra Victor, cleared takeoff, right turn, caution possible jet blast."

No daydreaming now. The centreline is almost as wide as our airplane, the rest of the asphalt peppered with skid marks. Once the tailwheel lifts off, the plane begins its drunken lurch, the centreline more elusive now, wide or not. Flight comes like sleep to an insomniac. The lurching stops, and the ground slowly, ever so slowly, drops away. This is no airliner.

On those rare days when the sea fog is only a thin softening of the western horizon and the smoke of pulp mills dissipates into gossamer wisps, the coast of British Columbia is transformed into a paradise. Few of life's pleasures can match the joy of shore-gazing from 500 feet up, mingling with gulls and eagles, watching killer whales and sea lions, and succumbing to the spell of the open ocean's drunken roll on the outer coast of Vancouver Island.

The aircraft is a theatre, and the scenes flash by in enchanting entertainment. Waterfalls spill out of the rain forest onto surf-sculpted rock. Sunbleached logs dance in the breakers like the rattling bones of dinosaurs. Rolls of foam chase a mob of sandpipers across a glistening beach. The show is intoxicating, and the silent movie flickers past the screen of the window; misty beaches, eerie rockforms, romantic lighthouses, cliffs and coves, shipwrecks and driftwood.

From a higher altitude the coast takes on a different character. The hinterland of Vancouver Island reveals huge tracts of brown clearcut areas riddled with tortuous logging roads, veins draining the lifeblood of the forest. Where second growth trees have appeared, the slopes are an even-textured light green, easily distinguished from the darker, rougher looking patches of remaining mature stands. On the whole island, there is only one small river valley whose forests remain as they have for centuries, but there is no guarantee that its magnificent cedars and spruces will not fall prey to the chainsaw eventually.

Throughout the inner coast, a glance out the window reveals a mountain kingdom of alpine lakes, sheer granite cliffs, and the most extensive glaciers found in southern Canada. The long fiords, locally called inlets, reach deep into the heart of the Coast Range, where mountains over 9,000 feet high rise straight out of pale waters laden with glacial silt. From the tidewaters of Knight Inlet it is only twenty-five miles to the summit of 13,104-foot Mount Waddington, the highest mountain wholly within the province. Once aptly called "Mystery Mountain," it presides over a mountain range that spends most of the year obscured in cloud.

The sheltered Inside Passage provides the main transport route not only for west coast Canadians, but for American domestic trade between Washington and Alaska. At any time of the year, the waters are alive with traffic of all sorts: container barges, self-loading log haulers, passenger ferries, luxury cruise ships, pleasure craft, ore carriers, and all manner of freight vessels. During fishing season, parts of the coast are literally choked with seiners, gillnetters, and trollers. At salmon season, Rivers Inlet or the mouth of the Fraser River are so jammed with boats one could almost walk from one shore to the other on their decks.

For those who know and respect the coast, it is remarkable flying country. Seaplanes are as basic to the region's transportation needs as buses are to the rest of the country, but regular planes not equipped for sea landings are more limited along this rocky coast. For the airborne sightseer who is fully aware of the risks involved and knows when not to take chances, flying along the B.C. coast is a joy that is overflowing with visual rewards. The newcomer, perhaps unprepared for the flood of scenes that will flow past his front-row seat, may find he has to return for a second or third showing. In fact, as he emerges from his airplane theatre, he may conclude that he could spend a lifetime watching the show and never see the same thing twice.

III If the great mountain ranges of western Canada could be rotated ninety degrees to lie on an east-west orientation, then perhaps the Pacific storms would track effortlessly onto the prairies, sharing their wealth of rain with the rest of the country. But meeting the mountain barrier at right angles, weather is forced to drop its load on the rain-forested western slopes in order to rise over each mountain range, and tumble over the leeward side, only to trip and stumble over the next range. The mountain atmosphere is reduced to chaos, with cloud and rain at higher elevations, and erratic turbulent winds in the valleys.

But weather is not all that is forced across this obstacle course. If history could be rewritten to suit the natural borders of geography, then logic would dictate that the Cordillera of western North America be the territorial boundaries of a single mountainous nation. Domestic transport and communications could then be established along the natural trunk lines of the major river valleys running north and south from the Gulf of California to the Arctic Ocean.

But these valleys have been of little use to the settlement of western Canada, and even the broad Rocky Mountain Trench has now been flooded for almost one-third its length, its transportation value forsaken for other economic considerations. Instead these valleys, like the mountains flanking them, are crossed successively by the east-west links that have helped define Canada, *a mari usque ad mare*. It has been a hard-won battle. Today, as in Canada's youth, the railways and highways must feel their way through the mountains, negotiating high mountain passes, dropping down into the valleys, crossing rivers, then climbing to the next pass.

Airplanes, one would assume, are exempt from this battle. But these mountains are no mere trifle, and a light aircraft is not at all exempt. In order to travel in a straight line, a cruising altitude of 12,000 feet is necessary to ensure ground clearance; to avoid the turbulence of mountain waves, 20,000 would often be preferable. For small, single-engined aircraft which normally fly by visual flight rules (VFR), these altitudes are impractical or downright impossible. Furthermore, visual flight is rarely feasible this high, since at altitudes of three or four thousand feet and up there is likely to be cloud for much, if not all, of the journey. There is little alternative, then, but to follow the time-honoured trade routes through the mountains, sticking close to the railroads and highways and hoping that the next pass will not be blocked by cloud. It is usually a rough ride. The turbulent valley winds can be at best the source of irritation and nausea; at worst they can tear the aircraft apart.

The passenger hoping to get that once-in-a-lifetime vista as he soars among the summits will perhaps be disappointed to find that his aerial view of the Rocky Mountain landmarks isn't so very different from the one from the Trans-Canada Highway. In fact, in places he will be so close to the Trans-Canada that his view may be confined to the bottom of his sick-bag.

But there are visual pleasures of mountain flying that are the exclusive preserve of the light plane passenger. In the right conditions he can cruise through the alpine world, riding a magic carpet that will present him with a close-up view of a mountain realm denied roadbound travellers. It is a rich world of sparkling jewels: a turquoise lake sleeping in the lap of a wildflower meadow, a herd of back-lit mountain goats strung like pearls along a ridge, or a glacier spilling iridescent sapphires of ice into the treeline. It is a treasure that can easily make him forget the lure of the snowy peaks that lie in misty seclusion far above his head.

IV The most fertile soil in British Columbia fills the lower Fraser valley like a deep green wall-to-wall carpet, neatly trimmed to fit the mountains on either side. Ahead of us the Coast Range and the Cascades converge on the town of Hope. The feeling is a bit like being pushed into a corner, the only way out of which is to enter the deep Fraser Canyon. Looking back at the miniature prairie stretching off to Vancouver and the Strait of Georgia, we start to monitor the sound of the engine more closely; flat fields suitable for emergency landing are becoming scarce.

Thu-whumph! Here we go, we're out of the smooth air of the valley. The jolt is followed by a series of little jiggles, and the altimeter needle finds a new spot a hundred feet from the old. To the left and down about a thousand feet are two gliders in tight formation, glued to the mountainside. The air in motion around Hope is their friend, their source of lift.

Thu-WHUMPH! They have lots of friends here.

The turn northward into the canyon starts out smoothly, but another gust holds the right wing down, then suddenly lets it go. It shoots up like your arm when you pick up something light that you think is heavy, and now we're banked too far to the left. A quick glance out the left window reveals a dizzy view of the top of a semi-trailer swishing along the wet highway. A shower must have just passed through.

The canyon is remarkably deep. We've been maintaining 5,000 feet, plus or minus (the altimeter is hard to hold steady), but outside the right window ponderosa pines blur by while down to the left, almost a mile below, a tiny orange cable car dangles over the boiling waters of Hell's Gate. The river which ran silky brown past the dairy farms of the lower valley is here a foaming white flume, the water draining from 89,000 square miles propelled through the mountains as through the nozzle of a fire hose.

Thu-WHAM! The camera bag jumps off the rear seat and an 85mm lens joins the coffee thermos under the front seat somewhere. An effort to retrieve it is impeded by a second thump that produces a bruise and some unprintable language in the headsets. It feels like we're riding the canyon in a barrel rather than an airplane, and the joys of flight are becoming soured.

But to take a more positive attitude, a trip like this will, if nothing else, vividly demonstrate that the waters of the Fraser are not all that tumble through the canyon: we are literally riding atmospheric rapids here, an invisible maelstrom of eddies and standing waves a mile deep. It can be as exhilarating as white-water canoeing, seeking out updrafts and free lift, waiting for the telltale thump in the seat of the pants that sends the altimeter around the clock.

But alas, the positive attitude is not all that easy to take when the tables turn and hard won altitude is snatched out from under the plane in one good slam. The pleasure of sightseeing dwindles away as the stomach demands more and more attention. The Fraser Canyon is notorious for such rides, and time becomes agonizingly drawn out, making it all the more difficult to notice the subtle change in the landscape. As the end of the canyon approaches you suddenly realize that the open, terraced, pine-studded slopes below couldn't be more different from the rain-forested mountainsides near Hope.

The broad interior plateau now stretches to the eastern horizon, wide open space inserted between two mountain worlds. The altimeter still flirting with the 5,000-foot mark, we are looking across the forested highlands at treetop level. The parched interior landscape known to highway travellers is found only in the river valleys incised deeply into the terrain, valleys which broaden gradually as we head east into the Shuswap and Okanagan country.

Whumph! The turbulence has diminished somewhat since the canyon, and is now much more the work of daytime thermals as the air boils off the searing dry earth. It's mildly irritating, but at least it's not debilitating, and window-gazing continues as the terrain builds dramatically into the Monashees.

Eagle Pass, at 1,841 feet, is not particularly high, but the weather is notoriously bad. This is the first dumping ground for the upslope rains. We're lucky there is a ceiling at 6,000 feet, allowing us to maintain our altitude as we enter the tunnel formed by cloud, cliff, and valley floor. Past the hairpin turn at Three Valley Lake, the pass is disconcertingly narrow. Despite the fact that we are over three thousand feet above the highway, the mountains off each wingtip reach into the cloud for another half-mile overhead. Even hugging the mountainside, we have to bank a little to be able to see the highway, out of view below the cabin floor.

Emerging from Eagle Pass into the wide Columbia River valley at Revelstoke is like being shot from a torpedo tube. We're suddenly very high over the town and its steeply-pitched roofs, gathering up courage in the open spaces to tackle Rogers Pass ahead.

The Selkirk Mountains were one of the great obstacles in the building of the Canadian Pacific Railway until Major Rogers finally found a pass through them. Had he been able to survey his route by air, he would not have found it any more readily. Approaching from the west on foot, as we are now by air, he stood literally at the brink of the pass, yet he didn't see it. But neither can we. The Illecillewaet River appears to lead us straight into a cul-de-sac, a box canyon flanked by mountains over ten thousand feet high. A quick glance down at the chart: there it is, a zig-zag line indicating the Trans-Canada, reassuring us the road indeed passes through the Selkirks here. For an instant we doubt the chart, there must be some colossal mistake . . . but when it is nearly too late to turn around, the highway veers to the left, leading into the pass itself.

Although we are at 5,000 feet, the Trans-Canada monument is a scant 700 feet directly below, ringed by camper trucks. We are completely surrounded by mountain walls, striped with avalanche tracks leading to the curious mogul mounds intended to discourage snowslides from blocking the highway. The railway is conspicuously absent here: on its climb up the Illecillewaet it bashfully darts in and out of snowsheds before disappearing completely into the mountains, safe in its tunnel from the thundering snows of the avalanche-prone pass. There is no sky visible in the windows now in level flight; even banking the plane steeply only reveals more rock above, and the feeling is claustrophobic. Another right-angle turn to the right and we emerge from the pass. Looking back to where the railway issues into the Beaver River valley, we are even more amazed that the route was ever found at all. There is nothing to distinguish this tributary valley from any of the others that penetrate the ramparts of the Selkirks.

Nature has a sense of humour. After negotiating one of the more spectacular mountain passes we now find ourselves crossing the same river that we crossed on the other side at Revelstoke. The Columbia carries less water here, but the valley it occupies is a good five miles wide. This is not the river's work, however, but the result of a fault line that has created the province's longest and largest valley — the 900-mile Rocky Mountain Trench.

The town of Golden winks in the sun, a comfortable half-mile below us. But we must gain more altitude now, since merely maintaining our 5,000 feet through Kicking Horse Pass would see us slam into the highway 320 feet below the summit. For light plane pilots, the Rocky Mountains present difficulty not in the height of their peaks, but in the height of their valleys. Past Kicking Horse Pass, the floor of the broad Bow River valley is 5,000 feet above sea level, and altitudes that would be a dizzy height over Vancouver are barely respectable barnstorming altitudes here.

The mountain landmarks around Lake Louise and Banff assume their familiar postcard poses, but the view is nonetheless breathtaking. At waist-level to the Rockies, we are afforded full-length shots of the mountains, and somehow this makes them even more impressive than from the ground. A full-length view of Mount Robson at a distance of a few miles, as one gets when flying through the Yellowhead route to Jasper, is a sight that completely defies description; it is not often one can gaze squarely at two vertical miles of rock, a head-to-foot portrait of the King of the Rockies.

By the time we reach Banff townsite, the mountain world has become a familiar object of aerial sightseeing. The tributary valleys have been passing to the side, one after another, steadily marking time as we peer up to their headwaters in the way bus passengers peek up city side streets, hoping to see something special — a waterfall, a glacier, or a still-frozen lake. It is a visual shock to peek around the last corner, past the last mountain buttress, to find the two-dimensional expanse of the prairies unfolding into infinity. The late afternoon sun throws shadows of the mountains forward over the foothills, arrows pointing off to the darkened horizon.

It is almost as if the wind has been held at bay by the mountains and now, unleashed in the foothills, it is hellbent on making up lost time on the prairies. In fact, that is not far from the truth. The air in motion that tripped and stumbled over the mountain barriers, tossing hapless airmen in its frustration, suddenly finds a complete lack of obstacles and a renewed, rabid strength. The relentless wind on the prairies is a constant headache to pilots. Even when luck puts a good tailwind behind you, you can be sure that landing at your destination will be hair-raising, particularly if you are flying a taildragger.

But from the point of view of sheer terror, wind alone is not the most significant weather factor on the prairies. As the brilliant blue skies of a summer morning gradually begin to fill out with cottonball cumulus clouds, the pilot can be sure the afternoon will bring all kinds of trouble in the form of thunderstorms.

A single thundercell is analogous to a large bubble rising from the bottom of a pot of water in a rolling boil. In fact, they are both caused by the same process: heating of the surface produces rising pockets of warmed air. The many-coloured ground that is the delight of the airborne photographer is a surface that absorbs the sun's rays unevenly, causing large differences in the rates at which air is warmed. It is therefore not uncommon to come across a single isolated thundercell over the prairies, a huge column of agitated air reaching to thirty or forty thousand feet. Such a monster will flatten out into an anvil of ice crystals at its head, while inside a witches' brew of hailstones is stirred around, the hail unable to fall until the stones are large enough to overcome the updrafts of 60 m.p.h. or more.

To fly directly through a thunderstorm would be like rowing a dinghy under Niagara Falls; the largest commercial jets have sophisticated miniature on-board radars installed specifically to detect them, and will detour miles around them. Thunderstorms are an awesome spectacle, like a meteorological Mount Everest (but Mount Everest is only a fraction of the size). Even from a distance of five miles or more, the wall of billowing dark cotton fills the windows, lightning bolts dance eerily within, and a huge skirt of prairie dust is blown up from the leading gusts about the base. Were it not for the implicit idiocy of being in the air near these things, it would be tempting to fly in gleeful circles around them, giddy with the sight of nature in a rage.

But having once been caught near a thunderstorm, airmen will go to amazing lengths to avoid them. The most effective technique is to rise well before dawn, and take off into the clear pink morning sky, long before the pot boils, even before the burner is turned on. On such mornings one can forget the anxiety and irritation of the afternoon turbulence, and turn one's attention to the bird's-eye view of a world coming awake.

And awake it does. If there is one word to describe the prairies, it is *busy*. Everywhere you look, the land is humming with the activity of feeding a nation.

Although not densely populated, the prairie provinces represent the single largest region in Canada that is continuously and completely shaped by the work of man. If art is the visual expression of human endeavour, then the palette knives of ploughs and combines have produced a collective masterpiece so monumentally vast that a single flight from the Rockies to the Shield will afford a viewing of only a tiny fraction of the canvas.

It is not a static painting either. Throughout the growing season the colours and textures change, from the furrowed dark of the ploughed fields of spring, to the even green of midsummer's foliage, and then to the fine-lined golden calligraphy of the harvest. From the aerial gallery we can watch the artists at work, each creating his portion of the montage with an individual style, and in dealing with his particular set of topographical and drainage problems, contributing to the endless variety of patterns, forms, and colours.

If there is any constraint on artistic expression to be found, it would be the regular north-south east-west grid of the surveyed sections. The neat geometry is unfailingly adhered to, even when applied to topography that seems unhappy with the superimposed order. The man-made divisions appear particularly incongruous near the badland areas along the Red Deer River in Alberta, where the drainage of rivers has cut deep incisions that disregard the squared-off fields, making you wonder if the farmer must detour a few miles to the nearest bridge in order to finish ploughing the back forty.

For aviators the grid is a ubiquitous compass, since the roads that delineate the squares run true north and east. This presents a bit of a Euclidean puzzle: true north lines must converge at the pole, but in order to ensure an honest section the roads run parallel, disregarding the earth's curvature. The puzzle is solved subtly by small jogs in the northbound roads, a bit of geometric legerdemain. The grid system even influenced the surveyors of the Saskatchewan-Manitoba border, which proceeds slightly east of south; about every twenty-five southbound miles, the border takes an easterly jog for a mile or two, making it theoretically possible for a Saskatchewan farmer to look northwest into his Manitoba neighbour's field.

Finding one's way across the flat expanse in an airplane is a bit intimidating at first, but soon each mile takes on its own character and features, making navigation quite easy. In doubt, one can always resort to using binoculars to read the names of towns on grain elevators, the airman's traditional roadsigns. Once the routine of picking your way across the map is established, you can gaze out to the landscape below and witness the ever-changing artwork come to life. You soon realize that those who feel the prairies are short of scenery just haven't seen them from above.

VI The wealth of Alberta is brandished in the fields below, oil wells growing like weeds in the fertile ground, spreading cattle ranches relaxing in the high morning sun. Calgary is swelling well beyond the city limits depicted on the latest aeronautical chart, its suburbs a sea of manicured lawns with a leading wave of housing construction. The new face of the economy mingles freely with the older agricultural one, from the highrises of downtown Edmonton, to the rigidly squared-off rapeseed fields around the city, to the clown-striped strip farms across the rolling shortgrass west of Lethbridge.

Hoping to climb out of the thermal turbulence was wishful thinking, it's just a bit too late in the day now. But the view from higher up reveals a mesmerizing array of field patterns, and the cooled air feels refreshing in the greenhouse of the aircraft. With the strong westerly wind, the flight to the Saskatchewan border has been short and the scenery restful. The badland area around Dinosaur Provincial Park looked particularly interesting, and we make a note to return at sunrise sometime, when shadows play across the dissected rock strata.

But ahead the cauliflower-top cumulus clouds foretell a bumpier ride, probably some showers, maybe even a Cb (cumulonimbus, weatherman's word for thundercell) or two. We'll have to keep a running check on Saskatoon weather. We're just crossing the road that runs along the border, and can see it head north to where it cleaves the town on the horizon into Lloydminster, Alberta and Lloydminster, Saskatchewan.

A glance at the clock: ten past. The hourly weather reports should be in now.

"Vermilion Radio, Zulu Sierra Victor, thirty south Lloydminster, VFR. Have you got the latest Saskatoon for us?"

"Sierra Victor, Vermilion. Saskatoon showing only scattered cumulus this hour, but we do have a pilot report, a line of Cb activity south of Battleford appears to be heading northeasterly . . . "

Sometimes you think it might be better not to know. Now the rest of the trip will be an anxious cat-and-mouse game with thunderstorms. It really takes the edge off sightseeing, but there isn't much we can do about it for the moment. So we let our minds drift off to the crazy pothole-studded patterns on the fields of western Saskatchewan, stealing a glance or two at the southeastern horizon where thunder lurks.

By the time we pass North Battleford there is a line of puffy cumulus cloud with anvil tops, ahead and to the right, stretching away to the south. Battleford Radio tells us that Saskatoon weather is still good, but now the ominous remark "Cb tops southwest" is added to the teletype report. The thunderstorms must be right between us and Saskatoon, just south of our path but tracking across it.

We edge over to the north side of the Saskatchewan River to try to keep a good distance. The black bases of the Cb's are visible now, with stringy veils of precipitation reaching to the ground and blotting it out. Even with our little detour, they seem to be positioning themselves between us and our destination, and it could be a close race.

"Saskatoon Radio, Zulu Sierra Victor, twenty-five northwest, estimating at three-five. Where do you paint the Cb's now?"

"Sierra Victor, Saskatoon. Radar has them one-five west, tracking northeast quite rapidly. Contact tower now on one-one-eight-three."

The line of cells seems to be not only crossing our path, but converging on us, making it touch-and-go whether we can outrun it. By the time we get past it, Saskatoon may be right under. To the left the sky is clear blue, and the river sparkles in the sun as it loops northward. To the right, and uncomfortably close, the rich prairie soil is thrown up into dust devils under the black wall of advancing cloud. The turbulence has escalated into terrifying slams, and the little Pacer is alternately in and out of control. A jolt of lightning flashes beside us, crackling in the headphones, and our mouths go unpleasantly dry. Saskatoon Airport, still in sunshine, comes into sight behind the edge of the first line of showers.

"Zulu Sierra Victor, Saskatoon Tower. We have some very severe weather to the west, it looks like it will be on us in a moment. Will you need assistance tying down when you get here?" Prairie hospitality.

"Negative, we just hope we can get there first, but I'd appreciate a short taxi."

"Sierra Victor, cleared to land one-four, wind one-five-zero at ten, gusting twenty. You can land on the grass if it would be closer to the ramp for you."

"We'll give the runway a try first, thanks."

As it turns out, we beat it by a good ten minutes, not even a squeaker. We push the Pacer into a tie-down spot, get some ropes on her, and then stroll over to the terminal building to watch the spectacle of a good prairie thunderstorm.

The show is over quickly, but we wait for a few hours in the coffee shop for the afternoon to cool down a bit and the isolated thunder activity to dissipate into evening. The day's cloud buildup has left us with a ceiling of 1,500 feet, so the next leg will be at low level. That's fine. The sights reel by faster and the more intimate view is revealing and entertaining.

Just out of Saskatoon, a field is being worked into a pattern so bizarre that we can't resist circling it a few times. The man on the tractor is so immersed in his work he doesn't notice us banking overhead, camera aimed out the window. We can't figure the logic in his wanderings, and we idly speculate that he's not really a farmer at all but the inventor of an unsuccessful tractor steering mechanism, and we laugh.

About a mile further a field in summer fallow is being turned under. A flock of birds follow after the plough, feasting on the easy pickings of the newly-exposed earthworms. They flutter around the tractor like gulls around a seiner at net-hauling time.

There is no break in the chain of glimpses stolen from a day in the life of the prairies. We even feel a twang of guilt for intruding, merely *being* there, albeit momentarily, in our privileged gallery. A battered pickup truck, mid-sixties, rumbles along a dusty road below. Alongside the road a row of windbreak bushes lead up to a house with a long driveway. As the truck approaches, a dog bolts down the driveway for the road, the sharp sound of his barking left to our imaginations, as in a silent Chaplin movie. The dog darts past the windbreak and the truck suddenly swerves violently into the left lane, then back again as it continues on unchecked, the dog tapering off behind. We roar with laughter in our headsets, wishing we had a movie camera.

The wheatfields of eastern Saskatchewan stretch endlessly on into Manitoba, broken only by grain elevators, tiny churches, barns, and isolated villages. The grain bows and undulates in the wind like seagrass in a tidal current, wave after wave fanning out in golden cat's-paws on a yellow ocean. Approaching Winnipeg, the terrain seems to redefine flatness, roads and railways scribed onto the drawing-table landscape leading into the heart of the city.

As we gain altitude to over-fly the downtown area, the capital city is utterly lost in the limitless expanse. The corner of Portage and Main is camouflaged under the grey angularity of the urban core, outdone hands down by the vibrant colours and zany patterns of the surrounding farmland. Winnipeg, like so many other cities in the country, is swallowed by its setting when viewed from high up. It comes alive from above only when seen at close range, close enough to peer between the tall buildings and down to the streets.

Not far east of Winnipeg, the glacial lake that once covered what is now the Red River valley has left its beaches to mark the end of the plains and the beginning of the Shield. The landscape is in transition here from smooth and easy to rough and difficult, from groundwater stored in deep soil to lakes perched on rock outcroppings, from western to eastern Canada.

Pitching our tents under the wing amid the mosquitoes and pine-scent of the cool air, we flash back on a blur of close-up scenes that blend into a composite picture of the prairies. Most of the scenes are small-scale and intimate: a backyard, a man and his machine working the land, individuals collectively providing food for the country. The composite is an impression of a land so *alive*, so full of human activity, that neither of us will ever be able to look at a map of western Canada and see emptiness.

VII The change from a treeless landscape bustling with human activity to a woodland wilderness is sudden and complete. Below is a watery expanse, seemingly more lake than forest, stretching continuously off to the horizon. The only signs of civilization are the single highway and the railway threaded through the trees and looped around lakes, barely visible unless viewed from directly overhead.

The ease with which one could get lost over northern Ontario is disturbing. The lakes are the best guides to navigation, but they don't necessarily look like their imitations drawn on the chart. This isn't to say the chart is crude or inaccurate; Canadian pilotage charts are in fact topographical maps with an overlay of aeronautical information, and are far more detailed geographically than are their American counterparts. But the trees, the sunlight, and the topography all play tricks on a lake's features, especially when viewed from an oblique angle, and in many places it is almost impossible to identify your position positively from visual clues alone.

Fortunately, however, it is easy to identify towns, since they are so few in number and are readily seen from afar. Dryden, Ignace, Fort Frances, Atikokan: if the plume from a nearby pulp mill is not visible, a large open pit will be. Even though the towns are widely scattered, it is not difficult to see the next one in the distance before losing sight of the last, provided the air is clear enough and you fly at a reasonable altitude.

But once the horizon fills out with the blue waters of Lake Superior, navigation is no longer a problem. From here on it is coastal flying, and the freshwater oceans beyond Thunder Bay create their own coastal climate. Fog and low cloud, of the likes not encountered since the B.C. coast, will now be the thing to watch out for. The onshore breezes pulled in from the lake by the heating of air inland will meet high terrain on the North Shore so that, rising, they will condense the moisture picked up on the hundred-mile journey across Superior. As a result, low cloud and rain will plague the coastline from Thunder Bay to Wawa, while fifty miles farther inland the sun may be shining. When the night air settles off the slopes and back out on the lake, it will be cooled by the chilly waters and once again condense, this time as fog.

This morning we don't seem to have waited long enough for the fog to dissipate completely, but what is left remains well offshore in benign wisps. The rugged beauty of this coastline is flattened somewhat at 5,000 feet, and we feel a slight twinge of envy for the cars winding their way along what must be a spectacularly scenic part of the highway. But that envy is easily suppressed; they cannot see the islands' pink rocky fringes melt into the deep azure of the clear water, or the Slate Island Light far offshore, wrapped in its cocoon of fog.

The air is smooth and the view relaxing. On the highway a string of cars worms its way around a headland behind a slow camper. An impatient sports car bolts into the left lane and takes four cars before an oncoming truck forces him to squeeze back into line. When the truck passes, he jumps back into the passing lane. We can look ahead about two miles, where there is another string of cars, and yet another ahead of that. We feel smug to be free of the highway, and any remaining envy evaporates.

The shore from Terrace Bay to Marathon is littered with pulpwood logbooms. The booms are quite different from those on the west coast. There the huge logs are rafted into orderly rows, sorted and graded by size and species; here the comparatively tiny logs are jumbled into a homogeneous mass, tightly contained by boomsticks linked end to end like sausages around the boom's perimeter, taking on amoeba-like forms. Neatly circular in storage, the booms, when pushed by a tug, are comically indented at the point of contact, like a balloon being pricked. When towed individually or in groups, the sausage-link skin is pulled away from the inside logs, and the whole thing becomes teardrop-shaped.

The weather is exceptionally clear, allowing us to travel fairly high and make good time. We decide to bypass Wawa and carry on to Sault Ste. Marie for fuel. A huge streak of defoliated ground fans eastward from the mine near Wawa, the victim of acid fumes carried inland by the onshore prevailing winds. The shoreline south is particularly colourful, not in the rock itself but in the underwater deltas of mineral-laden streams entering the lake.

The Algoma smelter at Sault Ste. Marie is a monochromatic rust colour, as if the entire plant were built from the dust of the iron ore it processes. We are on the doorstep of the industrial heartland of the Great Lakes, but we are still surrounded by broad fields where farms are etched into the forest. To the east the highway leads into mining country, where towns are marked by the brilliantly coloured mine tailings around them, colours ranging from blood red to bright yellow and vivid blue. The notoriously scarred landscape near Sudbury is a fantastic painter's palette from the air. The vibrant saturated colours combine in surreal forms and patterns, bringing a surrogate beauty to an otherwise marred wasteland.

We elect to proceed southeast over the islands of Lake Huron, a route to Toronto somewhat shorter than the Sudbury one but with more overwater stretches. The shoreline of Manitoulin Island is fringed with wave-sculpted rock shelves, whose pink dissected fragments blend gradually into yellow and green as they dip underwater. The long hop over to Tobermory on the Bruce Peninsula encourages us to maintain plenty of altitude, but there is no cloud ceiling to worry about today.

South of the Bruce Peninsula the air begins to thicken with industrial haze, and Wiarton Radio tells us that visibility at London is down to four miles. This is a phenomenon not seen in the West. Although there may not be a cloud in the sky, we can be forced to grope along nearly blind, especially flying into the sun. We decide to head down the Huron shoreline to Sarnia, where visibility is reported somewhat better.

Between Port Elgin and Sarnia is mostly dairy farmland, but there is also industry of a staggering proportion. The nuclear power plant at Douglas Point, still under construction, is an immense complex that takes over a minute just to fly past. Around Sarnia, the entire landscape is constructed of steel and asphalt; row upon row of chemical storage tanks, a network of piping, a forest of chimneys, rail cars, and tanker trucks offering an inadequate reference for scale.

From here eastward across the heart of southwestern Ontario, the land has been touched everywhere by man, but in a way quite different from the bold patterns carved onto the open prairies by solitary farmers. Here the fields are smaller and more numerous, the many roads are lined with buildings of a wide variety, and the broad deciduous leaves soften the texture and blur the detail of the patches of forest.

As we move onto the Niagara Peninsula the trees arrange themselves into prim orchards. The region's number one scenic attraction is marked by a white plume ahead, rising out of seemingly featureless terrain. It is not until we are almost upon them that the falls are visible, spilling the contents of Lake Erie into the gorge they have cut back from Ontario's lakeshore. It is a thrilling sight. As we bank over the brink of the falls, we can see hundreds of figures crowding the lip, like lemmings about to jump. The photographer's boom mike follows his camera into the slipstream, and the roar in the headsets provides an ersatz sound track to the thundering spectacle. A circular rainbow straddles the billowing cloud of spray, our shadow a meagre dot in its centre. It is difficult to leave the falls, the temptation to remain a minute longer always there. But when we have had our fill, we proceed along the Golden Horseshoe to Toronto.

We pause over the Dofasco plant on Hamilton's waterfront, and watch as hoppers of glowing molten iron are shunted into cooling chambers, from which clouds of steam puff up as from a volcano. Like the plant at Sault Ste. Marie, the entire area is coloured rust, and heat from the steel mill is shooting thermals at us like flak, jolting us about in the air.

Halfway between Hamilton and Toronto, Oakville has affluence written all over its suburbs, tree-shaded houses punctuated with turquoise swimming pools. The Ford factory lies just ahead, its parking lots paved with newly painted cars in rows like beadwork. This marks the edge of the control zone for Toronto International, and as the radio dial lands on frequency the headphones burst into a chatter of voices from yet-unseen aircraft in the adjoining airspace. We crane our necks around for traffic; sightseeing becomes a passenger's privilege now, as the pilot concentrates on establishing contact with air traffic control.

"Zulu Sierra Victor, Toronto Tower. Radar contact, cleared eastbound along the shoreline, not above three thousand, report the four stacks." No words are wasted, and the instructions rattle off his tongue. The temptation to blurt out an acknowledgement is suppressed until each part of the message is noted.

We enter the control zone long before the haze reveals any sign of the city, but to the left the airport itself seems to mark the boundary of the metropolitan area. Just south and east of it the land explodes into suburbs, the freeways colliding in a tremendous tangle.

"Zulu Sierra Victor, Island Tower now, one-one-eight-two."

In the haze ahead a vertical string of strobe lights flashing in unison draws attention to the previously unnoticed CN Tower, now visible as a dark stiletto shape in the murk. The rest of the city is a cluster of angular block shapes silhouetted against the silvery lake. The radio knob is snapped onto Toronto Island frequency.

"Zulu Sierra Victor, Island Tower, good afternoon sir. You're cleared downwind left hand for three-three." The voice is so friendly you could shake hands with it.

"Island Tower, ZSV. Okay if we take a swing around the city for some pictures first?"

"Sure, no problem. Stay as long as you want, let us know if you want to go above two-point-five. Give us a call when you're ready to come in." No stern, this-is-serious-business tone to his voice, just the cheerful professionalism of a man who appears to enjoy his work.

For a moment it seems they've put background music on the frequency, perhaps to match the joviality of the controller, but then we realize the music is breaking into the aircraft band from the powerful commercial transmitter in the CN Tower, now just out the left-hand window. We turn tightly around the tower just above the level of the top observation deck, and proceed around the downtown core. It's a dizzying, fleeting view of rooftop ventilators blurring by close-up, and of traffic and rush-hour crowds far below. It's impossible to try to see everything at once, for everywhere is motion; cars turning, fountains flowing, and people, hordes of people in every nook and cranny of the city. We reel off several rolls of film in two passes, but the light is fading and the haze is killing the colours. We'll have to try again some other time.

"Sierra Victor, you're cleared to land three-three, wind three twenty at five to ten."

A flock of geese scatter as we cross the runway threshold. When the nose comes up the city towers over us in the windshield.

"Sierra Victor, Island Ground. Take it into the line in front of the tower there, you'll find a spot by the blue and white Cherokee. Where are you from?"

"Today we came down from Thunder Bay. We left Vancouver last Saturday."

As he keys his microphone, a whistle can be heard in the background. "Hmmm. That's a pretty good trip."

VIII The first sight of a city from above is a wondrous new awakening, an exhilaration of the senses akin to that felt by a farm boy on his first midway ride. To the airplane passenger, the street scenes and routine of urban life that have been dulled by familiarity are suddenly a great spectacle, and the urge to point and shout at the recognized places is overwhelming: "Look, there's the Science Centre!", "Look at the cars on the 401!", "There's our house!"

Never mind that they have spent their lives here and know every street. They have never seen it from above, and they are seeing it again for the first time. There is an intangible fascination in picking out the known and the recognizable, and fixing their coordinates in the total picture in a way that was previously not known and not recognized: "Wow, the school looks so close to home!", "I didn't know the park was so big!" From the air, the mundane becomes exciting, and the ordinary exquisite.

Something in the back of your consciousness refuses to acknowledge that the little diorama out the window is real. The city is your toy, and you are the omniscient observer: "You down there in that car, you don't know that on the next street men are working, and you will have to detour. But I know, I *see* it." Ignoring the triviality of the scenes you witness, you enjoy a sense of all-seeing power. The use of traffic helicopters to tip off rush-hour motorists was an inevitable development in urban aviation.

Over a city the photographer experiences his most frantic moments in a plane. Over farmland or forest, images present themselves at a leisurely pace and unexpected visual gems can command full attention; communication with the pilot is relaxed, and composition and exposure can be experimented with freely. In intervals between interesting subjects the boredom can be so acute that often making sandwiches becomes a welcome challenge.

But near urban areas, the number of possible images comes at him at an exponentially accelerating rate, like being sucked into a whirlpool. Almost without warning he finds himself looking out both windows at once, fumbling with lenses that vanish under the seat, reloading cameras that seem to empty themselves of film at precisely the moment when an exciting prospect appears. City images are detailed, fleeting, and complex, and demand the most care in framing and composition — a contradictory situation. The second and third pass turn up new possibilities, and the photographer reacts with intuition and guesswork, making split-second decisions about lens, filter, framing, and which side of the plane to shoot out of, all the while trying to confer with the pilot (who is invariably preoccupied with air traffic control) about manoeuvring the plane into the right position.

And still photographs cannot convey the motion, the kinetic energy, that envelops the city. It is something like the swarming of flies, like Brownian motion, but not as random. There is chaos in the whole, but there is order in the components: pedestrians passing on sidewalks, cars starting and stopping at lights like the coils of a Slinky Toy and flowing around interchanges like corpuscles in capillaries. It can be comical or it can be mesmerizing, but the motion is always present, and always in the foreground.

Montreal and Toronto together account for a fifth of the nation's population. These cities are to the Canadian urban landscape what the St. Elias Mountains are to the natural landscape: they fill the senses and perplex the mind. They are built by man but are beyond human proportion. The downtown cores of massive office towers and department stores are not oversized to the altered scale of the airborne eye; the real vexation is in the sea of suburbs, industrial parks, shopping malls, railyards, expressways, parks, and airports that surround them. Man, a six-foot creature that appears as a mere fleck on this ocean, has created a complex, ordered environment that covers the landscape, engulfs it, defines it.

Ottawa appears markedly smaller from the air, partly because it *is* smaller but also because its buildings are larger. The monoliths that house government institutions are everywhere throughout the city, shuffled in with the hotels, universities, museums, and office towers. There is an importance about them, even from the air, that annunciates the nation's capital. The Parliament Buildings are unmistakable, surrounded by moats of rigidly manicured lawn, presiding over a city held up as a national show-piece.

The cities, large as they may be, are still only isolated dots on the overall picture of southern Ontario and Quebec. To drive from Toronto to Montreal one need never leave the freeway, nor be very far from the nearest McDonald's; but the view from the car window is misleading, for the narrow band of civilization clings tenaciously to the highways that, in turn, parallel the St. Lawrence and Ottawa Rivers. From above, we can see where the rocky soil of the Canadian Shield has limited settlement to the fertile valleys. Flying from Peterborough to Ottawa is for all the world like flying north from Sudbury or Timmins; beyond the Ottawa River there is no significant change in the landscape until the wetlands leading to the shores of James Bay.

IX "Zulu Sierra Victor, left turn when airborne, report the Mercier Bridge at one thousand five hundred." The controller at Dorval Tower is authoritative, one of the few we've come across who assigns altitudes to visual traffic.

"Dorval, Sierra Victor at the Mercier Bridge. We'd like to circle the downtown area before proceeding en route."

"Sierra Victor, that is approved. Maintain fifteen hundred at all times. We have Bonanza traffic also downtown at two thousand. Report leaving the zone at the Lafontaine Tunnel." Even a rigid-sounding controller has flexibility. We can't recall a controller ever denying a request, even in the largest cities. There have been some delays in busy airspace, of course, but never a flat refusal to let us photograph something interesting.

Fifteen hundred feet turns out to be a perfect altitude to circle downtown Montreal. It's a bit low for comfort near the Place Ville Marie or the Stock Exchange Tower, perhaps, but the nearby remains of the Victoria STOLport offer a reassuring emergency landing spot. At the tunnel we free ourselves from the regimen of the control zone, and circle some colourful oil storage tanks in east end Montreal before heading for Quebec.

The St. Lawrence lowlands possess a bold graphic quality, a fantasia on the strip farms of French Canada. Seen from above, the difference of these farm patterns from those on the prairies is among the most telling expressions of differing cultural values. The western farmstead typically stands alone on its quarter section, a lone monument to the rugged individualist. But the more gregarious Quebecois have opted to remain close to neighbours and relatives, their houses clustered along the road and their fields extending back from the road in long strips for a half-mile or more. The system has the important advantage of providing river frontage, albeit only a short one, for each field. The fields are oriented away from the river, emanating from it like balsam needles from a twig. Bends in the river are negotiated with variations of elongated trapezoids, as farms of one orientation mingle with farms of another. In some cases the fields radiate from a central village, this carry-over from old world France producing a sunburst design on a pin-stripe backdrop.

Twenty miles southwest of Quebec we switch to Tower frequency. The radio comes alive with traffic, most of which is in French.

"Quebec Tower, Zulu Sierra Victor." The phonetic alphabet is supposedly international, but right now it sounds self-consciously Anglophone, enough so that the controller responds without hesitation in English.

"Zulu Sierra Victor, Quebec. Bonjour. Cleared to the circuit left-hand, report downwind." The ease with which he switches language is amazing to unilingual ears, but words are secondary to controllers; their thoughts are in numbers and the spatial arrangement of radar blips.

The French have, in typical fashion, brought a degree of poetry to the language of aviation. Somehow the expression *takeoff* is weak compared with the more descriptive *décollage*, literally translated "to come unglued." Such word imagery is carried to exaggerated lengths sometimes, and it was inevitable that the accurate if unwieldy term for flaps, *les volets hypersustaintateurs* (hypersustainers of flight), would be given up for *les flaps*. When orders are being barked to copilots low on final approach, brevity counts.

We taxi up to the gas truck at Quebec Airport, and engage in a mildly successful if disjointed conversation, in broken French, with the fuel man. His English turns out to be far better than our French. From here it is a long walk over to the terminal building for a bite to eat, and a check on the weather for the flight to Gaspé. The little posters that normally hang in Flight Service Stations — "Prepare and Prevent or Repair and Repent", "Caution is not cowardice, nor carelessness courage" — are here replaced with "English or French . . . the choice is yours, the pleasure to serve you is ours."

The weather is reported good all the way to Gaspé, and the irritating haze that hangs over the city here shouldn't extend much farther than Rimouski. Fully topped up with fuel and lunch, we repack ourselves into the Pacer and taxi out to the runup area. The magnetos are checked, controls moved through their full travel, seatbelts fastened, *les flaps* lowered a notch, and we are ready to come unglued.

From the air, Quebec must be the most colourful city in the country. Each rooftop, particularly along the tightly packed crooked streets of the inner city, is a bright colour — red, blue, yellow, green. The details of the buildings' old world architecture are etched into the texture of the city, delineating it as in a fine-lined pen and ink drawing.

Downstream of Quebec the St. Lawrence gradually takes on the appearance of a long bay, the river banks become coastline, and the mudflats give way to rock. The farms which filled the lowlands are now only a narrow band clinging to the shoreline, being squeezed into the river by the mountains on both shores. Beyond Rimouski there is but a single road along the water's edge. The string of farm houses thickens periodically into villages, invariably flagged by the presence of an ornate church which dwarfs the community.

The river no longer runs through a region, but instead now separates two distinct regions. Past Pointe des Monts the north shore takes an abrupt northward turn to Sept-Iles, where the river becomes the Gulf of St. Lawrence. Besides being the point where the lakers relinquish their cargoes of grain to the deep-sea freighters, Sept-Iles is also the terminus of the Quebec North Shore and Labrador Railway, and serves as the gateway to mineral-rich Labrador. In its dual capacity as grain and ore terminal, Sept-Iles is second only to Vancouver in terms of tonnage handled by a Canadian seaport.

Even on this sparkling clear afternoon, the north shore recedes out of sight over the horizon as we keep to the south shore, following the Gaspé coast around to the northern fringes of the Maritimes. The gaily painted houses below stand in the open, fully exposed to winter gales, on fields that have been cultivated for centuries. The storms of December seem remote on this warm summer day, but the fishing villages still have an austere quality that speaks of the people who live and work here.

As we round Cap Gaspé we decide to circle Percé Rock for some pictures in the early evening light before landing for the night at the town of Gaspé. The cliffs north of Percé are glowing red embers in the sun hovering over the Gaspé highlands. The rock itself, although we've never seen it before, is a familiar landmark posing in the silver water, but from above the green lawn growing along its backbone is an unexpected splash of colour. The air over the rock is peppered with seabirds, white flecks that swarm around it like bees around a hive.

The change from the locks of the St. Lawrence Seaway to the shores of the Gulf has been gradual, but as we pitch our tents under the wing the realization sinks in that we have now flown from coast to coast; last week we were flying around Vancouver Island, and tomorrow we will be exploring the Atlantic provinces.

Leaving the rugged cliffs of the Gaspé coast behind, we climb out over Chaleur Bay. The New Brunswick shoreline stretches away to the south, a long chain of pink sandy beaches broken only at Miramichi Bay. The sands dip under the inshore lagoons and resurface as salt marshes, their colour subtly blending with the green seagrass in the shallows to produce a pastel underwater fantasy.

Inland of the salt marshes, the New Brunswick forests reach uninterrupted to the western horizon. Although all but two Canadian provinces touch upon salt water, the Maritime Provinces are the only ones that deserve this name. With the exception of the communities along the Saint John River valley in New Brunswick, most Maritimers live near the coast, and virtually all settled areas are within twenty miles of the sea.

From the enticing beaches at Kouchibouguac National Park we turn east over the twelve-mile-wide entrance to Northumberland Strait, toward the western shore of Prince Edward Island. There is no subtlety to the colouring here; the pink sands of New Brunswick were only an appetizer for the deep brick red of the sandstone cliffs, repeated both in the topsoil and in the surf breaking on the beach. The colour is set off by the rich emerald green of the potato fields extending right up to the brink of the cliff.

We succumb to the urge to scoot along the water's edge at low altitude. Pickup trucks on the beach below the cliffs are being loaded with Irish moss, while horses drag carts out into the russet surf to pick up another load, waves breaking over them at shoulder height. Overhead the green crops bow to the onshore breeze and wave to the rolling red earth.

The inshore waters of Malpeque Bay on the north coast reveal underwater patterns that resemble those on the New Brunswick side, but with colours much more rich and exaggerated. The dunes of the outer sandspits are lightly topped with greenery, and the sands are fine, a pale sun-bleached rust. At Cavendish Beach there is a ludicrous explosion of humanity. The comic-book colours of pinwheel umbrellas and zebra-striped bathhouses are sprinkled among the reddening sunbathers who litter beach and surf alike.

The colours reverse themselves on the rambling hills of the island's interior, with green predominant in the farms and the brick-red roads supplying the trim. The prevalence of agriculture and the undulating topography recall the fields of western Saskatchewan, but much scaled-down. And from even a modest altitude, the sea is always visible, for there is no place on the island province that is more than ten miles from the shore.

It is only a very short hop across the narrowest part of Northumberland Strait to Cape Tormentine, and then to Moncton. The relatively small distances between cities and provinces in the Maritimes are a psychological relief after the vastness of the rest of the country. This gives us an illusion of mobility, despite our modest (for an airplane) speed of 110 m.p.h.

The communities between Moncton and Saint John shy inland from the Fundy coast by a good twenty miles, and it is little wonder; the shoreline for fifty miles east of Saint John is a rugged wilderness of steep cliffs with virtually no harbours. The south shore of Fundy is similar, but the fruit-growing belt of the Annapolis Valley lies only five miles inland behind a barrier of low hills, and the Annapolis Basin provides a good harbour at Digby. Only at the head of the Bay of Fundy, at Chignecto Bay and Minas Basin, do farms and villages rest by the water's edge.

This is one of the country's most visually spectacular landscapes from above. We have timed our flight to arrive over the Avon River mouth at low tide, and the effort is well worth it. Below us the miles of red-brown mud, exposed by the enormous Fundy tides, are dissected into eerie dendritic patterns incised into the luscious smooth texture by water draining off the slick flats as it chases after the receding sea. The patterns are bold and well-defined, as if someone had taken a huge branch of a dead tree and thwacked it into the muck, leaving its silhouette cast in the glistening seabed. Higher up on shore deep green tufts of grass delineate the high water mark, their graphic shapes negatives of the branched drainage gullies. Brightly painted fishing boats lie on their sides farther up the river, waiting for the tide to set them free.

The Fundy shore is a marked contrast from Nova Scotia's Atlantic coast, only fifteen minutes' flying south. As we fly out over Mahone Bay the water is crystal clear, the sand brilliant white, and the rocks pale pink. Everywhere the activity of seafaring people is evident. The town of Lunenburg is ringed with wharves cluttered with fishing vessels of all sizes. The town itself is a picture postcard, the neatly rowed streets lined with gingerbread houses painted rainbow colours, one of the prettiest towns we have seen in all of Canada. Out in the bay, dories painted as bright as the houses share the deep blue backdrop with the white flecks of sailboats.

Before landing at Halifax Airport, we circle the largest city in the Maritimes. The colours of Lunenburg put the typical grey buildings of downtown to shame, but the city has not yet bowed to the impulse to build fifty-storey skyscrapers. There is a conspicuous splash of colour at the container port at the harbour's entrance, where variously coloured loads are being lifted aboard a ship by one of three huge red and white gantry cranes.

The large airport at Halifax is often busy, but right now the controllers are relaxed and are chatting casually with pilots.

"Zulu Sierra Victor, Halifax Ground. Take it left on taxiway alpha, you should find some eighty octane at the flying club. Don't know your registration . . . you're not from around here?"

"One of us is from Montreal, one of us from the west coast."

"Long way from home in either case. How do you like this part of the country?" It isn't the first time we've been asked that question. Everyone feels his part of Canada is unique, a special place worthy of special admiration. And everyone is quite right.

"Beautiful. Really beautiful." The answer is weak, incomplete. There isn't any place between here and Vancouver Island that doesn't deserve that answer. We've just flown over four thousand miles of beautiful country.

And we are once again over beautiful country early the next morning, as the arms of the Bras d'Or Lakes embrace Cape Breton Island in the low sunlight. Today may be the day we can finally get to Newfoundland, but only a check at the Sydney weather office will tell.

"And what can I do for you today?" There's nothing like a sunny morning to bring a smile to a weatherman's face.

"Well, how does it look over at Stephenville, VFR?"

His smile fades. "Oooo, going to the Rock, eh? VFR?" But then he recalls the day's prognostic chart, and hope returns. He turns to the teletype and tears off a sheet. "Let's see . . . Stephenville . . . visibility *forty* miles, well, that's a switch. St. John's, ah, looks good. Deer Lake . . . St. Anthony . . . well I'll be . . . I ought to frame this! The whole province is wide open. It sure isn't often. You're lucky to get a day like this for VFR."

"Well, we tried to time it this way. Any new systems coming our way?"

"They show a front crossing New Brunswick today, looks like it will be here by tomorrow morning. Likely all of Newfoundland will be back in fog tomorrow, but today is good."

Newfoundland is without doubt the most difficult province in the country to reach in a light single engine airplane. One route is over only twelve miles of water at the Strait of Belle Isle, at the island's north end. This would be a very sensible route were it not for the fact that it is so difficult to reach from the mainland. From Sept-Iles it is over four hundred miles to St. Anthony, well beyond our safe fuel range, and the Quebec coastline leading to the Strait has few airports, no weather information, and no fuel. A detour is necessary, then, north from Sept-Iles to airports at Labrador City, Churchill Falls, and Goose Bay, leaving only a 200-mile leg south to St. Anthony. This detour makes for shorter stretches between airports, albeit over remote Labrador wilderness.

But even if the island of Newfoundland itself were not the goal, the mainland portion of the province offers sights that are well worth the detour. Beyond the mountains north of Sept-Iles, past the mysterious embroidery of the Labrador string bogs, the spectacle of Churchill Falls astounds the air traveller lucky enough to see them. A natural spillway for the Smallwood Reservoir, the falls are not always evident. Only at times of surplus are waters diverted from the generator's turbines to plunge into Bowdoin Canyon, sending a plume of mist high enough to sprinkle the windscreen of an aircraft circling a thousand feet overhead.

The only other route to the island accessible to light planes is the one we are trying today: from Cape North on the tip of Cape Breton Island across Cabot Strait to Port-aux-Basques, seventy miles of open water. The only way to minimize the risk is to climb as high as possible, so that we are beyond gliding distance from shore for only a short time, or at least so that we can be sure of finding a ferry or other boat to put down next to if the engine quits.

Weather will make or break a light plane trip to Newfoundland. Getting to the island itself is only half the battle; finding good visual flying weather while there means finding a place free of fog, by no means an easy task. With the surprised endorsement of the Sydney weatherman, then, we are fortunate indeed for the day's cloudless skies.

We leave Cape North behind as we climb to 9,000 feet. The distant Newfoundland shore is now visible on the horizon, and the thin white line of the Magdalen Islands can be seen floating on the Gulf of St. Lawrence, eighty miles to the west. The radio operator at Sydney Flight Service watches over us like a den mother across the strait, and hands us over to Stephenville long before we are out of his range. Below, a tiny wake streams behind the Port-aux-Basques ferry, a reassuring dot on the blue expanse.

When we are within reach of shore, we descend for a closer look at this hard-to-reach land. The beaches and villages along the coastline are pure Maritimes, but the high plateau extending inland looks for all the world like a piece of the Arctic. Descending further below the level of the high terrain, we can pick up on more of the character of the landscape: the weathered but still brightly coloured houses, standing exposed on the treeless, rocky soil; the cheerfully painted fishing dories pulled up on the beaches.

Taking advantage of the sparkling day, we decide to head north along the west coast to explore the spectacular scenery of Gros Morne National Park. At 3,000 feet, we are not far above the near-tundra of the plateau ten miles inland, and from this vantage the treeless terrain appears nearly flat. But as we approach the first of the park's three glacially-deepened valleys, the land drops away with heart-stopping suddenness a half-mile to the sinuous lake nestled between the rock walls. For a moment we feel an uncontrollable urge to scream and then we remember we are in an airplane and realise we have not been flung out helpless over the abyss. We circle once over the lake before continuing to the other side, where the sheer cliffs reach up to restore us once again to low altitude over the plateau. Progressing north, each valley is deeper, wider, and longer than the preceding one, and the beauty is overwhelming.

At the third chasm, we dive between the walls and follow Western Brook Pond out to the coastal plain, a low sandy barrier that prevents the sea from reaching the valleys, which would otherwise be fiords. From here we follow the rugged western shores south again over the isolated fishing villages, houses and boats always bright splashes of colour on the austere coast. Their colours seem redundant next to the blue and green of the sea, and the browns and reds of the rock, but the admonition of the weatherman reminds us that they are most often the only colour seen here. "Likely all of Newfoundland will be back in fog tomorrow . . . " In a land frequently obscured in grey, the times that visual flying is possible make optimists out of passengers.

At Stephenville we touch down in our tenth province in as many days. A single flight across the country can show us so much, yet so little. Each mile along the way reveals something new, but also poses many more questions. No matter how much of Canada we may explore, there is always so much more.

XI The altimeter concedes another thousand feet, creeping past the seven thousand mark, the dial difficult to read in the blinding glare. Outside a blue-white world of snow and ice and rock slips past the windows at a hundred miles per hour, yet motionless, time in suspension. The Kaskawulsh Glacier eases into the valley behind us, luscious ribbons of moraine blended onto its surface, fudge-ripple ice cream thawing in the summer Yukon sunshine.

The St. Elias Mountains are hung in the windows, abstract works of art, with shape and form, but without size. At 8,000 feet now, the engine gasping for breath, we're scarcely at knee level to the mountains. At 9,000 feet, at 10,000, it seems to make no difference. At 11,000 feet we are higher than the little Piper has ever taken us before, yet we are crawling along the floor of the mountain range. Ahead and to the left, Mount Logan basks in the sun, thirty miles away, just outside the window. We have to bank the plane steeply to the right to lift the wing, so that we can look at the summit, the highest point in Canada.

The mountain, like the country it reigns over, is immense, one of the largest mountain masses in the world. At this distance it fills our view, yet it would require another fifteen minutes' flying to reach its base, and twice that time to fly around its circumference. The mountain is a recluse, and despite its proportions it finds ample privacy in the vastness of the Icefield Ranges, which in turn hide under Canada's largest system of alpine glaciers.

At the head of the Donjek Glacier we turn northeast to follow its escape from the icefield. Descending more steeply than the aircraft, the frozen river dives over abrupt slopes and breaks into fragments, huge seracs and deep crevasses, blocks of ice the size of office buildings. The lower reaches of the glacier form an icescape of fractured blue iridescent chunks, sprinkled with pulverized rock and melting into brilliant turquoise pools. We are a good three thousand feet over the tongue of the Donjek, yet without the familiar clues of trees and buildings there is no telling how high we are, nor how large the glacier or the valley it fills.

We must cross the next ridge in order to fix the scale. The snow in the upper Burwash Uplands gives way to the late summer tundra, and then to trees. The thin golden thread of the Alaska Highway weaves its way along the shores of Kluane Lake, and tiny cones of dust chase after toy trucks. Off the right wingtip, Dall sheep are grazing in sociable gatherings. While the memory of the Icefield Ranges is still fresh, we try mentally to superimpose these signs of life, subscales for reference, on that dimensionless expanse.

Kluane National Park, despite the fact that its awesome mountains are hidden from view from the Alaska Highway, is within the most accessible area of Canada's North. Not only has the highway brought road traffic north of 60°, but its very construction established a series of airstrips leading northwest from Fort St. John, B.C. Some of these have become important airports. For the Pacer and other aircraft of modest range, these facilities make casual travel to the North possible; the southwestern Yukon is the light plane's gateway to the Arctic.

It is the gateway to a much different Arctic, however, from that of the east. Climate and geography have been relatively kind to the western half of the continent. Trees are found at low elevations throughout the Yukon and along the Mackenzie River, beyond the arctic circle to the shores of the Beaufort Sea. Dawson, a thriving city during the gold rush, lies farther north than Frobisher Bay, yet the locale of the latter is much more "arctic" than the forested hills around the Klondike.

There is no mistaking Dawson's status as an historical town; the preserved buildings, the wooden sidewalks, the old bank whose vaults daily received deposits of gold sacks, the stern-wheeler propped up on the river bank (a requisite for every self-respecting Yukon community), all are clearly distinguishable from above. But the gold rush has left a more widespread, far more permanent mark in the adjacent Klondike River valley, one that commands more attention from an overhead airplane than does the town itself. The dredges that followed the gold-panners into the valley have literally left no stone unturned; they have systematically uprooted the stream bed and redeposited it in long rows of scalloped mounds that wiggle over the valley floor like giant worms. The sight is startling and even a bit revolting, as if we are viewing the intestines of the disembowelled Klondike.

North of Dawson, we follow the Dempster Highway past the Tombstone Mountains towards the arctic circle. Autumn is beginning to wash pastel colours over the landscape, and the magenta cast of bearberry is broken by the bright yellow of poplars spotlighted in the clean sun of late August. In another week or so the ground will be ablaze with warm colours, dusted lightly by the icing sugar of the first snowfall.

The Dempster Highway meanders lazily over empty land on its way to Inuvik. The lack of people does not mean, though, that the land has not been touched by man. Scars repair themselves very slowly in the North, the limited topsoil and vegetation barely able to recover from even a single disturbance. The indelible records of the infrequent visits of surveyors and prospectors over the past few decades have gradually compounded. Bulldozer tracks and seismic lines criss-cross the area like the canals of Mars, covering huge tracts of land in the Peel River basin and surrounding the sensuously beautiful Richardson Mountains on the Yukon-Northwest Territories border.

Beyond the Richardsons the Mackenzie Delta stretches off to the Arctic Ocean on the horizon ahead. The country's largest river is not content to end its 2,635 mile journey by merely dumping its waters unceremoniously into the ocean; instead it bursts into flower some hundred miles short of the Beaufort Sea, blooming into the most intricately detailed landform on the continent. Lakes appear as islands on a sea of muskeg, connected by causeways of meandering river channels. It is a lacework of unparalleled complexity, the fluvial swan song of a great waterway.

The size of the Mackenzie River is brought home to us only when we fly up its length to Fort Simpson. From Inuvik it is an all-day trip, with a fuel stop at Norman Wells. Navigation is easy along the broad river, but the journey seems interminable as the river leads us through the forest fire smoke surrounding the Franklin Mountains near Wrigley. By the time we leave the Mackenzie to head south to Fort Nelson, we have followed it for six hours yet have covered only a quarter of its length.

From Fort Nelson we follow the Alaska Highway south to the Peace River district and land at Dawson Creek, Mile O of the highway. For southbound road travellers this is the beginning of civilization, the place where air cleaners are changed and the dust is washed from cars. Our airplane, too, carries its memento of the North, and when we climb out of the Pacer at Dawson Creek airport we have to brush out the considerable collection of black-flies lodged between the windshield and the panel.

XII The September sun hesitates momentarily over the mountains of Vancouver Island, casting its last sprinkling of red over the masts of freighters lying at anchor off English Bay. The lights of the city appear one by one in the twilight, as we circle lazily over downtown Vancouver before returning to the airport. It is our last flight, and we want to prolong it indefinitely, but darkness is spreading into the streets below.

Remnants of the rush-hour traffic are moving steadily over the bridges, headlights spraying the pavement with tiny fans of yellowish light. Directly below, a crowd of pedestrians is released from the sidewalk and surges across Georgia Street, whose streetlights point off westward to the twinkling sea of suburbs. Beyond the lights of Burnaby the darkened Fraser valley is almost imperceptibly green in the growing blackness, and beyond the valley the pink ghost-images of mountains reflect the last of the setting sun.

It is all one panorama: the pedestrians, the street, the suburbs, the valley fields, the distant mountains. By turning our heads, we can see it in a continuum, humans to mountains to the black eastern horizon. Beyond that horizon are more such scenes, personal yet grand, intimate yet comprehensive. Our airplane has put together for us a composite picture of the country, complete of detail and magnificent of size.

On the seat beside us is a stack of charts, bearing familiar names, familiar places. Before we left we had some idea of what we would find on the land they depict. But for the most part, our journey has been an exciting series of discoveries. It has given us a picture not only of what a region looks like on a large scale, but of what its people are doing on a human scale. We have been high enough to see whole landscapes from above, yet close enough to see them from within.

When we look at a map of Canada, we can see how much more there is. There are places we will never be able to fly over in the Pacer, and many more we could get to but probably never will. That still leaves a lifetime of flying experiences for us to enjoy. Looking at the large areas on the map that we may yet see from above, we can speculate on what they contain, what they look like, and how huge they must really be. But we know they will also contain unexpected details that cannot be mapped, and proportions that cannot be imagined.

The city is ablaze with lights now, and the Strait of Georgia is a platinum grey beyond the airport.

"Zulu Sierra Victor, Vancouver. Cleared to land runway twelve, short of zero-eight."

The approach lights shine amber onto the underside of the wing, flooding the cockpit with an orange glow. We float down the runway, delaying contact with the ground, the excuse being that we have to turn onto the taxiway at the far end. The main wheels bump onto the pavement with a squeal, and we lurch to the left, then right, and the tail comes down ever so slowly.

"Sierra Victor, keep it rolling across zero-eight, left at the end, ground one-twenty-one-seven when clear."

Turning between the rows of blue lights, we bob up and down in our seats as the springy undercarriage exaggerates the bumps on the asphalt.

"Zulu Sierra Victor, Ground. Cleared on alpha to the south ramp. Your flight plan is closed."

Opposite: Canada has by far the longest coastline of any country, with fifteen per cent of the world total. For just the small portion of this which is regularly travelled, an extensive system of navigation aids is required. This unmanned light beacon marks Cape Tryon on the north coast of Prince Edward Island.

Opposite: For four-and-a-half centuries, the flow of European history up the St. Lawrence has often passed within sight of Percé Rock, monument guarding the entrance to a nation. The quarter-mile long limestone megalith is a seabird sanctuary, and contains an estimated four hundred million fossils. Stark evidence of the power of time and the ocean, the rock was once an integral part of the mainland.

Above: Known only to local Indians just a century ago, Lake Louise is probably the world's most famous mountain lake. Like hundreds of other lakes in the Rockies, it owes its creamy turquoise colour to suspended rock flour, the finest particles in the silt brought down in the meltwater from grinding glaciers.

With the water in places two storeys deep where it rolls over the
edge, Horseshoe Falls blasts out a plunge pool deeper than its
hundred-and-sixty-foot height and undercuts the rock at such a rate
that within a human lifetime it retreats upstream a distance greater
than its fall. Three hundred years ago, when Niagara was first seen by
Europeans, the brink would have been at the top of this picture.

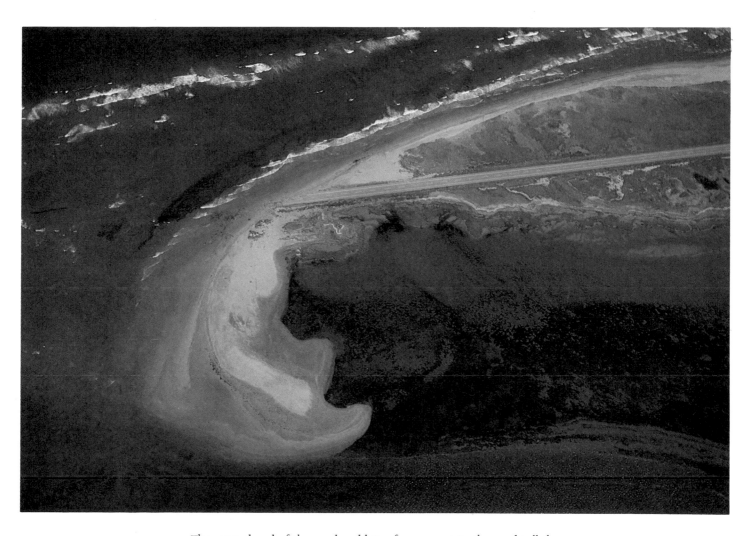

The ragged end of the road and bits of pavement in the sand tell the
story. Prompted by a stray hurricane, in one day the sea remodelled
the west tip of Rustico Island, part of the usually hospitable beachland
of Prince Edward Island National Park. The highway, meant to cross
the harbour to North Rustico, proved to be insignificant.

Above: Conspicuous in autumn, a small clump of aspen finds enough
moisture along a stream bed to thrive in the midst of the prairies near
Pincher Creek, Alberta.

Opposite: Carved by water erosion rather than glaciation, the west
slopes of the Richardson Mountains in the Yukon mark the edge of
the only extensive region in Canada that was not touched by the Ice
Ages. A patch of bearberry, already bright autumn red, is visible near
the centre of this view, taken in late August just north of the arctic
circle. The photo provides a surprising perceptual illusion when
looked at upside down.

Overleaf: String bog in southwest Labrador resembles an attractive
weave from the air. An obstacle to travel on land or by water, the
muskeg formation consists of strands of moss half-floating in shallow,
dark brown water.

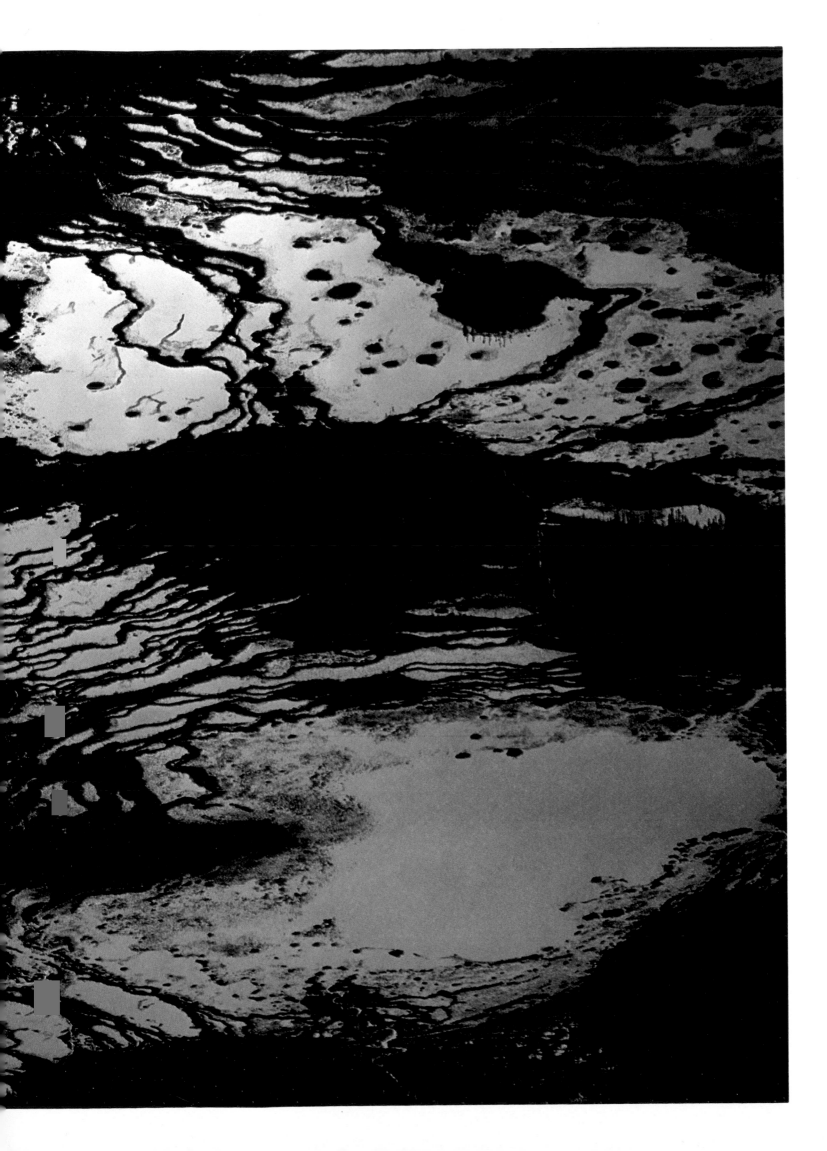

Opposite: Viewed from straight overhead, an unnamed peak on the Dewar Creek/White Creek divide in the southern Purcell Mountains of British Columbia is delineated by the late afternoon sun. The east side of the mountain sinks into deep shade; the southwest flank basks in the strongest light; spruce and autumn-gilded larch cast long shadows in the alpine basin at left; and the north-facing slopes preserve the most of an early-September sprinkling of snow.

Above: Twice as high as Niagara, Helmcken Falls on the Murtle River have carved an impressive cauldron out of the layers of lava which underlie much of Wells Gray Park in British Columbia. Thick slabs of debris-covered spring snow linger inside the pit.

Above: One of the world's spectacular natural wonders, taken for granted by Canadians but utterly astonishing to visitors from most other countries, is the annual saturation of entire forests in vivid, brilliant colours. This small segment of the great autumn tapestry is in the Ottawa River valley, near Rigaud, Quebec.

Opposite: A strikingly unusual landscape when first seen from the air, open boreal woodland, or lichen woodland, is in fact quite common. It covers half of lake-studded Labrador and New Quebec. What looks like greenish snow is actually caribou moss carpeting the ground around widely dispersed black spruce trees.

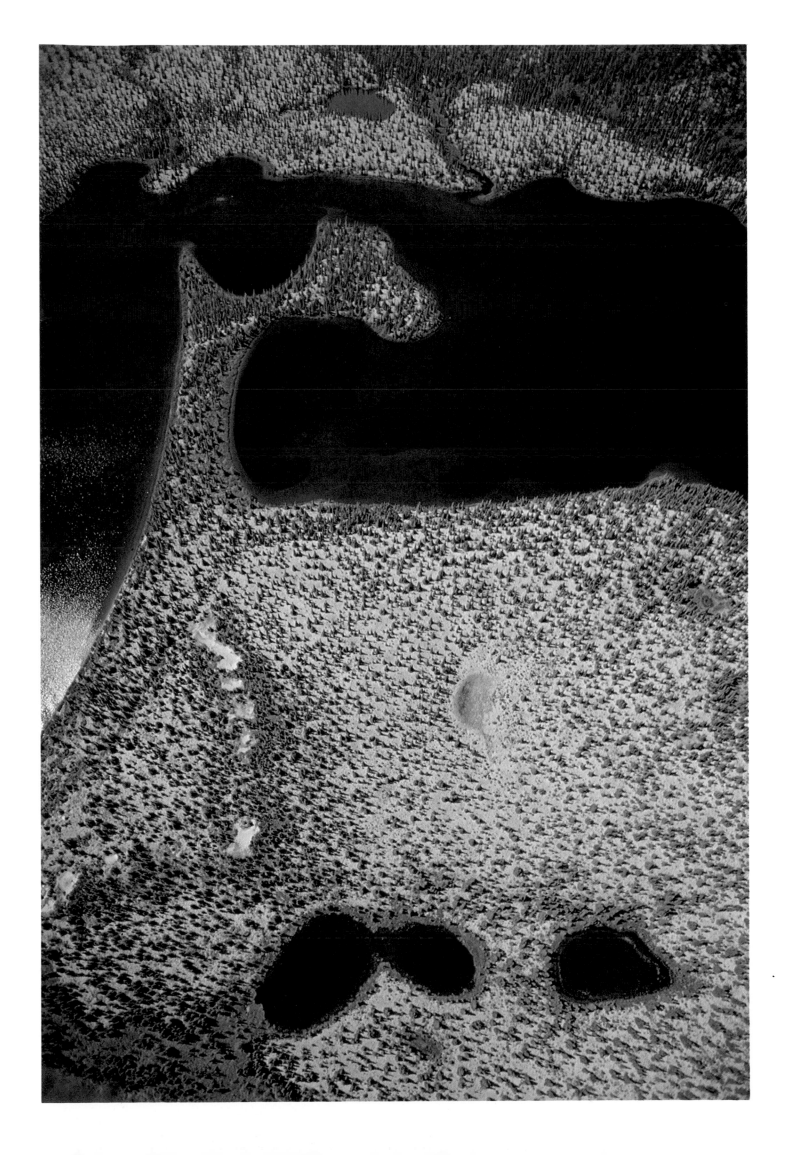

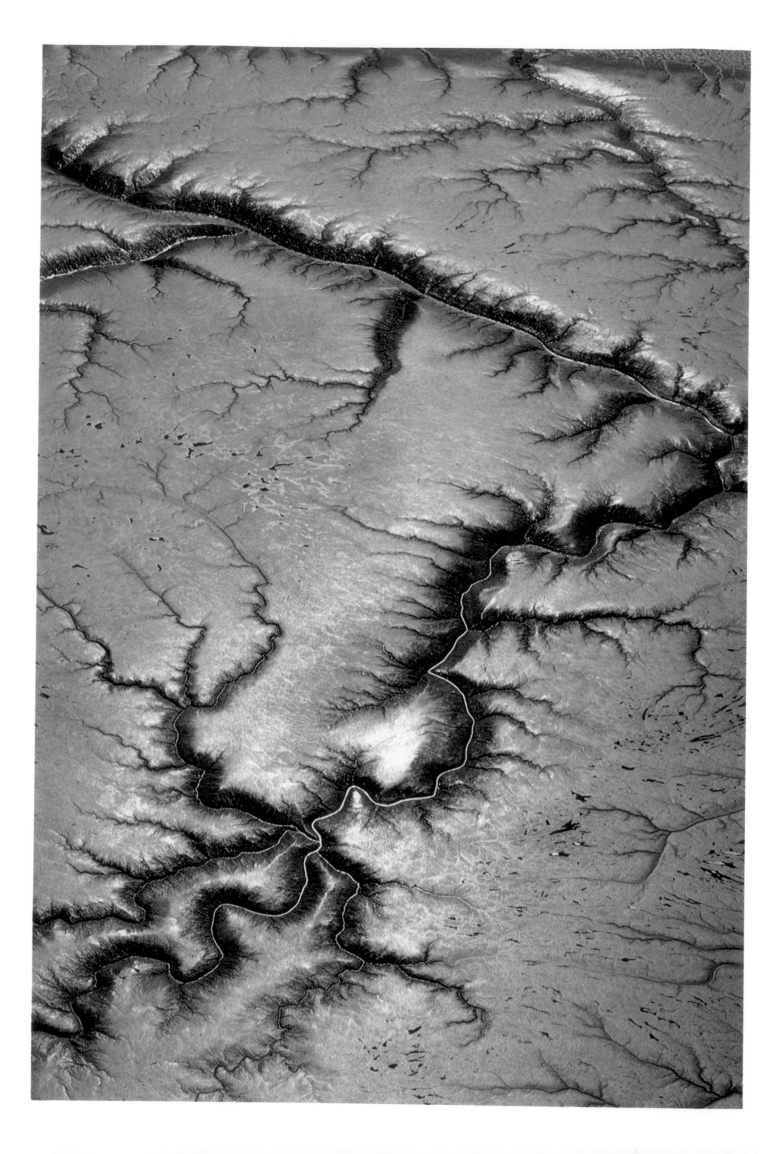

Opposite: Here appearing a platinum turquoise, the mud flats of Minas Basin lie exposed for miles during low tide at the head of the Bay of Fundy. The tides here are not unequivocally the highest in the world; a maximum range a foot-and-a-half greater than the fifty-three feet frequently cited for Fundy has been recorded in Leaf Basin, off Ungava Bay in northern Quebec.

Above: While the east has the world's highest tides, Canada's west coast has the world's fastest tidal currents in places where large inlets lead to the sea through narrow openings. The boat-wrecking whirlpools of Skookumchuck Rapids, seen here on an outgoing tide, reverse themselves four times a day and disappear during slack water when the waters of Sechelt and Jervis Inlets are briefly in equilibrium.

Above: Opaque with the suspended remains of pulverized mountains flushed from melting glaciers, the Slims River stirs itself into Kluane Lake, the largest in the Yukon.

Opposite: With over half of the earth's fresh water covering a total area the size of France and Great Britain combined, the Canadian landscape everywhere displays the myriad patterns of water. In this view of a portion of its delta, the Goulais River slides into Lake Superior, the largest body of freshwater in the world.

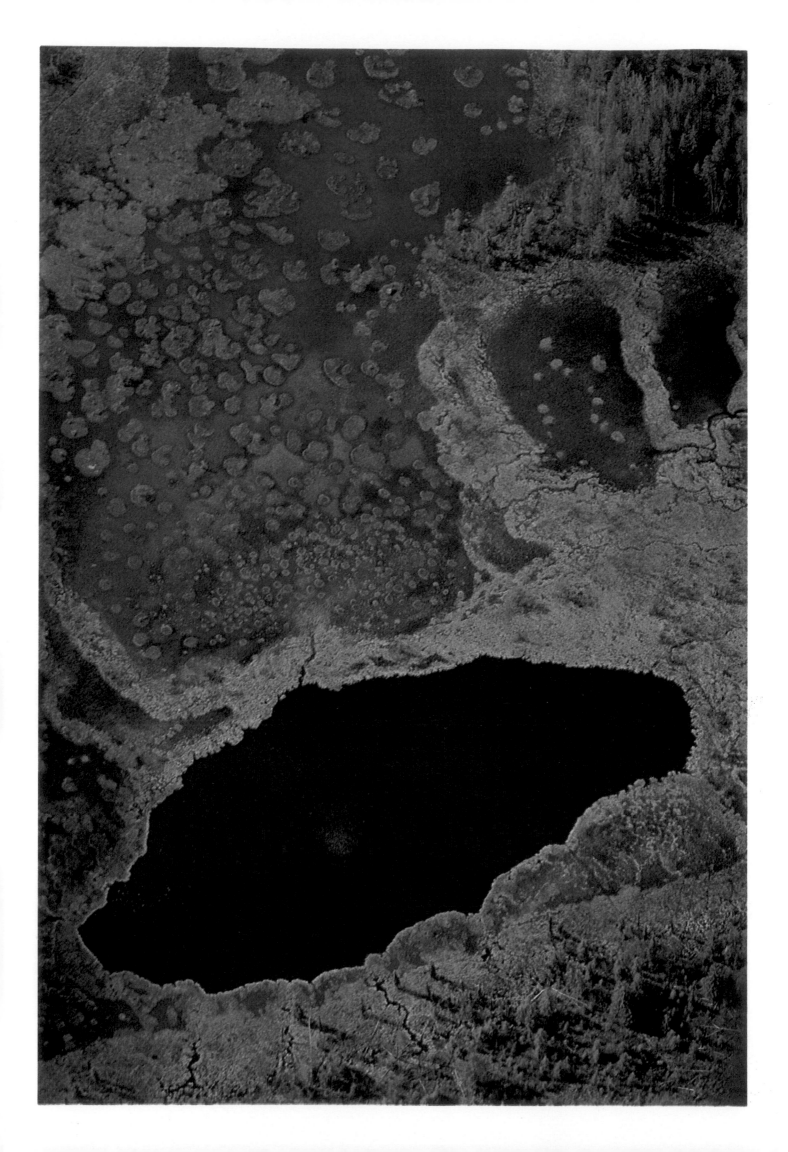

Opposite: A spring-brown marsh encircles a pond in the Murtle River valley, Wells Gray Provincial Park, British Columbia. Once much larger, the area of the pond is continually reduced by accumulating vegetable matter, which turns the pond into marsh, then meadow, and finally forest.

Above: Shunted about by wind and tidal currents, one of hundreds of ice floes drifts in Pangnirtung Fjord, Baffin Island, in August. The surface of such sea ice is a source of fresh water in a salt water environment.

Above: The Mackenzie Delta comprises tens of thousands of lakes and ponds interwoven with thousands of miles of stream channels over an area more than twice the size of Prince Edward Island. This view looks southwest up the East Channel to where the Kalinek Channel diverges, and beyond that to the large, main Middle Channel.

Opposite: The Thirty Thousand Islands, whose name considerably understates their actual number, pepper the east shore of Georgian Bay for a hundred miles. They constitute the largest archipelago of freshwater islands in the world. The wakes of pleasure boats stitch paths across passages which once sheltered the canoes of Jesuit missionaries and fur traders.

Opposite: An oil derrick claims a piece of farmland west of Calgary. While there is only one chance in ten, on the average, that the drilling rig will strike a productive deposit, the potential payoff is tremendous.

Above: Like giant pills, petroleum storage tanks are arranged inside the huge refinery complex in the east end of Montreal. The orange pipeline brings in crude oil from tankers berthed along the nearby St. Lawrence.

Overleaf: The pulp and paper industry, one of Canada's largest, uses great quantities of water (the materials in this book required six hundred pounds of it). Most mills have water treatment ponds for oxygenating the polluted waste. Whipped by large aerators, the foamy effluent curves into suggestive forms which, from above, are as visually seductive as they are aromatically repelling. This evocative pair was photographed at Fort Frances, Ontario.

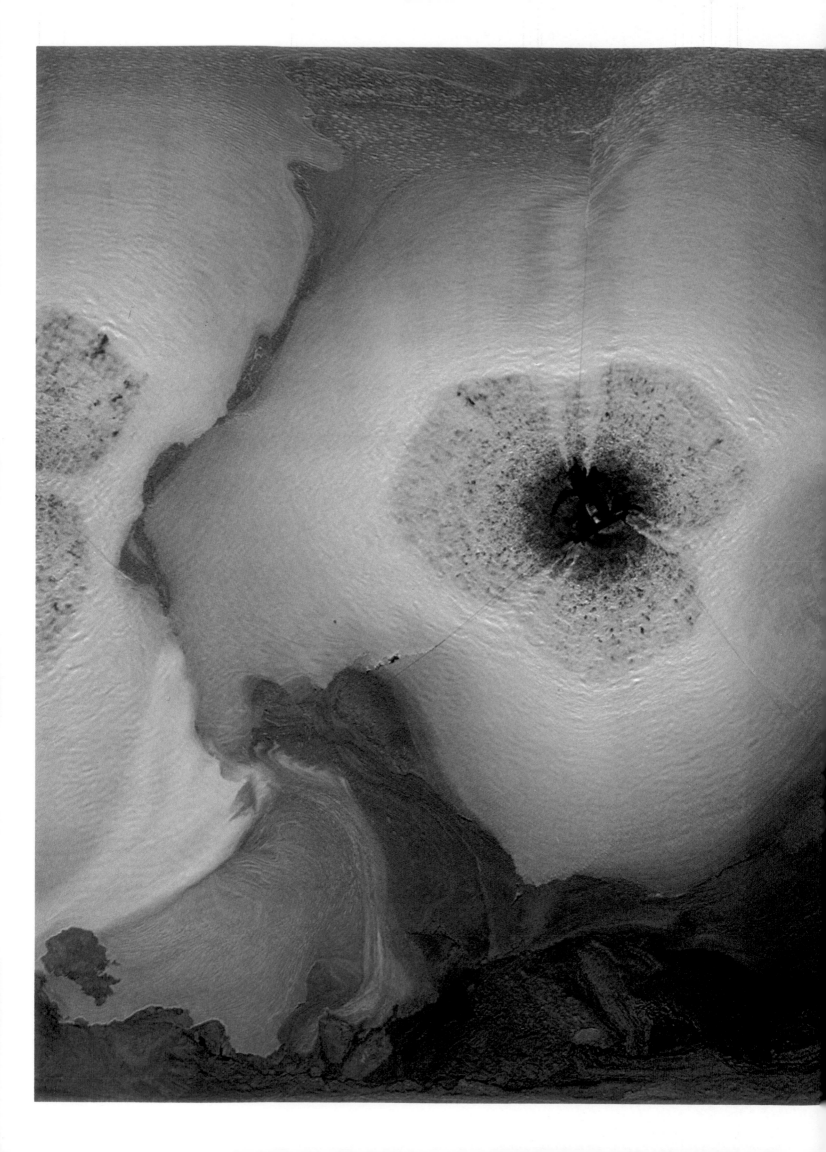

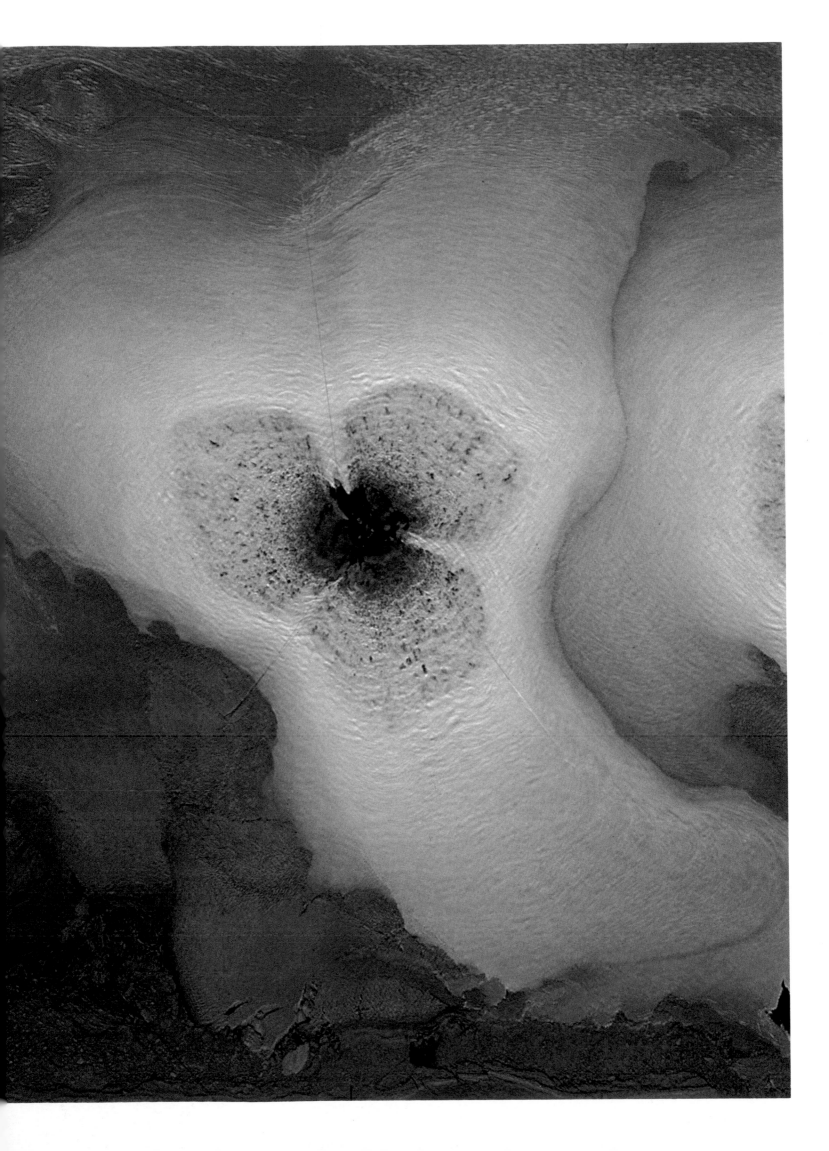

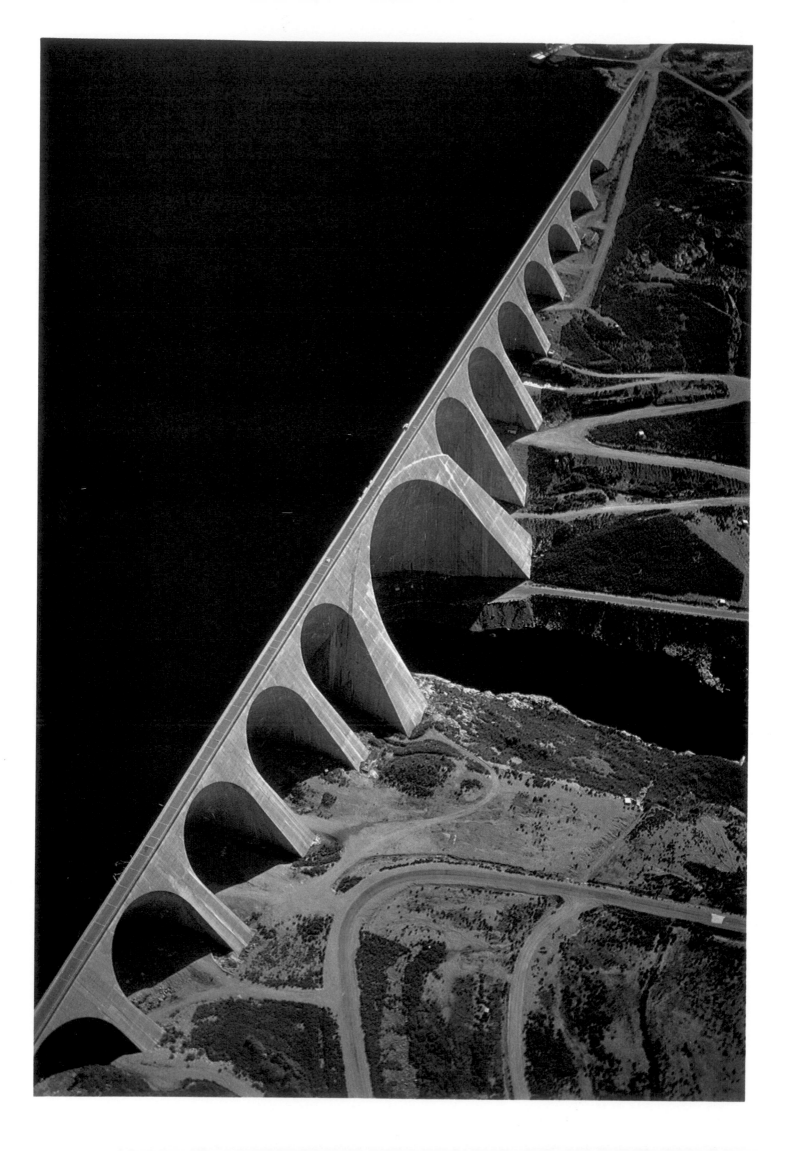

Opposite: The graceful concrete arch buttresses of Manic 5 (officially, the Daniel Johnson Dam) belie its massiveness. A mile long and seven hundred feet high, the remote northern Quebec dam is the largest example of this type of construction in the world. The central arch alone would span Montreal's tallest skyscrapers.

Above: Exactingly assembled from more than eleven thousand individual pieces, some weighing as much as a hundred automobiles and each fabricated at a site thirty miles away, the Olympic Stadium required precast concrete engineering unprecedented in scale and precision. In terms of size and proportion, the resulting interior space is one of the most spectacular anywhere.

Above: The wastes spilled out from mines and mills often reveal extraordinary abstract designs when viewed from above. These tailings are near the copper smelting centre of Rouyn-Noranda.

Opposite: Tallest in the world, though not the biggest, the Sudbury smokestack serves the world's largest nickel smelter, which processes ore from nearby mines that have been the world's most productive source of the white metal since the beginning of the century. The records and superlatives are all sadly tarnished: the stack has also been the world's largest single source of acid rain.

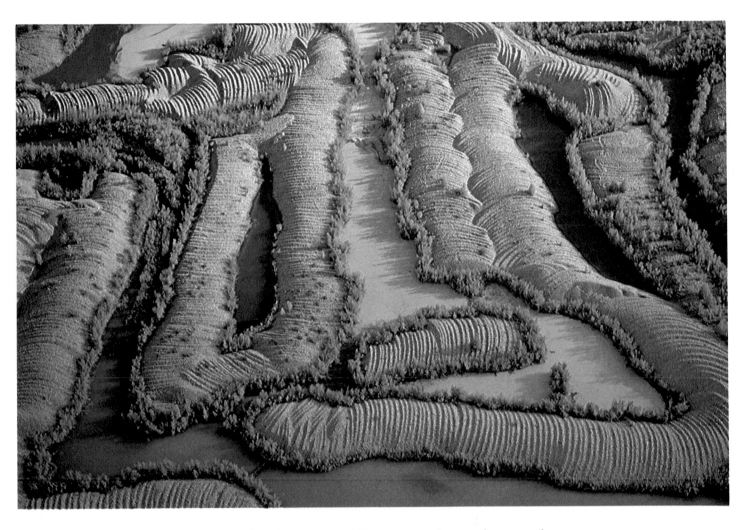

Opposite: Tailings from the world's largest potash mine dominate the landscape near Esterhazy, Saskatchewan. Potash has been discovered deep under the Saskatchewan prairie in deposits large enough to last the world several thousand years. The watery salt wastes, separated by flotation and conveyed from the mill, evolve into an enormous abstract canvas.

Above: Above Dawson City, miles of wormlike tailings testify to six decades of determined burrowing for gold along the alluvial flats of the Klondike River. Ten years after the Yukon gold rush, individual claims were no longer profitable and were consolidated to be worked by large floating dredges which churned through several thousand cubic yards of gravel each day.

Above: Hauled onto frozen lakes and rivers during the winter, the forest harvest of eastern Canada begins its long float to the mill when the ice melts. Here hundreds of acres of spruce and balsam logs on Deer Lake in Newfoundland await the spring pulpwood drive down the Humber River to Corner Brook, where the world's largest integrated pulp and paper mill turns out a thousand tons of paper every day.

Opposite: Abundant rivers provide the most economical transport for the fine pulpwood harvested from the slow-growing boreal forests of the Shield; but where a hydroelectric reservoir bars the way, tugboats must shuttle the logs across the long stretches of flat water. Containing many thousands of logs eventually destined for the mills at Baie Comeau, Quebec, this pair of purse booms is towed across the reservoir behind Manic 2 Dam.

Farmland east of Montreal in May clearly displays Quebec's distinctive type of land division known as the rang system. Property was originally distributed so that each settler had access to a river. The resulting long lots became even narrower when a father divided his farm amongst his sons. When the riverfront was all occupied, another rang, or row of lots, followed beyond the first.

Creating a superficial resemblance to the layout of Quebec farms, dryland farming in the prairie provinces — conserving moisture by planting only every other year — is done in alternating strips on the same farm in order to prevent wind-drifting of soil. In these fields south of Calgary, the grey strips are bare earth in summer fallow; the gold is ripe wheat; the green is unripened grain. Combining has begun on a swathed strip across from the farmstead, while the strip at the top of the picture has been completely harvested.

Above: North of Calgary, a field is deliberately fired in spring to eliminate the straw left behind by the preceding season's combining. Not good practice — it destroys organic material in the soil — firing is sometimes done for disease control, or when it would be too difficult to work the straw into the earth.

Opposite: Good farm hands are not always easy to find. Pretty to look at, this unusual pattern in a rapeseed crop near Tofield, Alberta, reveals a several-thousand-dollar mistake: during planting, the fact that one of a tandem pair of tractor-towed seed drills wasn't dropping its tiny dark seeds apparently went unnoticed for too long.

Opposite: Near Lacombe, Alberta, at the beginning of September, the top layer of a field in summer fallow is turned in order to eliminate weeds which would otherwise use up moisture from deeper soil. After first tilling around the green wet areas, the farmer crosses them with his implement raised to avoid getting bogged down. Contrary to first appearances, he has not started in the middle of the field: the surface of the soil tilled the previous day has dried.

Above: Guided by the tracks of two pivoting irrigation systems, swathers have cut (but not yet harvested) wheat into a mesmerizing pattern north of Lethbridge, Alberta. Unusual both in overlapping and in their diameters of two-thirds of a mile (half a mile is the norm), the circles maximize coverage of an awkward size field exactly one mile long but less than a mile wide.

Overleaf: Traced around the dark drainage ditches, a swathed wheat field near Drumheller, Alberta, is reminiscent of op art.

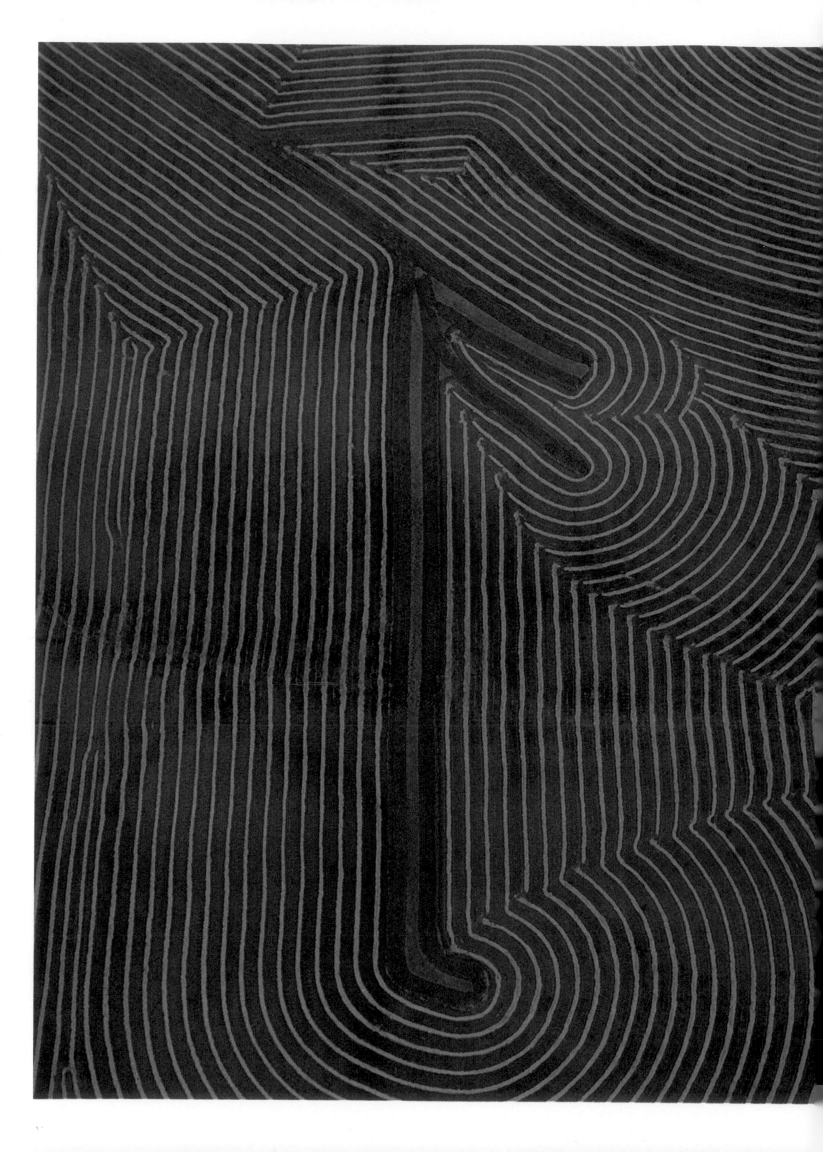

In heavily irrigated southern Alberta, where the fields are usually one
mile square, crops are frequently raised in large circles, this shape
resulting from pivotal irrigation systems. Swathed grain covers half of
this field near Brooks at the beginning of September. The green half
contains a partially cut second crop of alfalfa, destined for cattle feedlots.

Climate and rich black soil make the Rolla-Landry District near the
Peace River the best grain farming land in Canada. This wheat field is
being swathed perpendicular to the direction of the prevailing wind
and the direction in which it was seeded, in order to promote quicker
drying of the rows of grain.

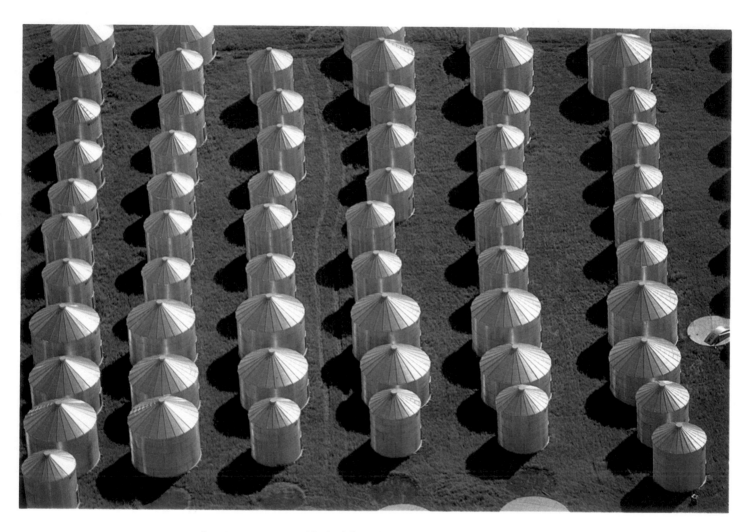

Above: Here preassembled, although on-site assembly is more usual, grain bins each worth several thousand dollars wait in a dealer's lot near Ponoka, Alberta. Their principal function is on-the-farm storage; but they are sometimes used for drying or preserving grain by having warm or cool air, respectively, circulated through perforated bottoms.

Opposite: One of the continent's largest container ports is located at the eastern terminus of the CNR at Halifax harbour. Two straddle carriers are visible at the top of the picture, organizing the containers and shuttling them to and from the mobile straddle cranes that service the trains or to and from the huge cranes that load and unload the ships.

Above: Operated by Canada's largest private corporation and largest private real estate owner, the Canadian Pacific freight yards in Winnipeg are among the most extensive anywhere.

Opposite: Bound for Vancouver harbour, a unit train exactly ninety-eight cars long — the maximum length sidings will accommodate — crawls up the flat valley of the Athabasca River just inside the east entrance to Jasper National Park. Composed of a string of identical cars, unit trains provide the most economical means of land transport for freight such as wheat, coal, ore, containers, potash and — in this case — sulfur.

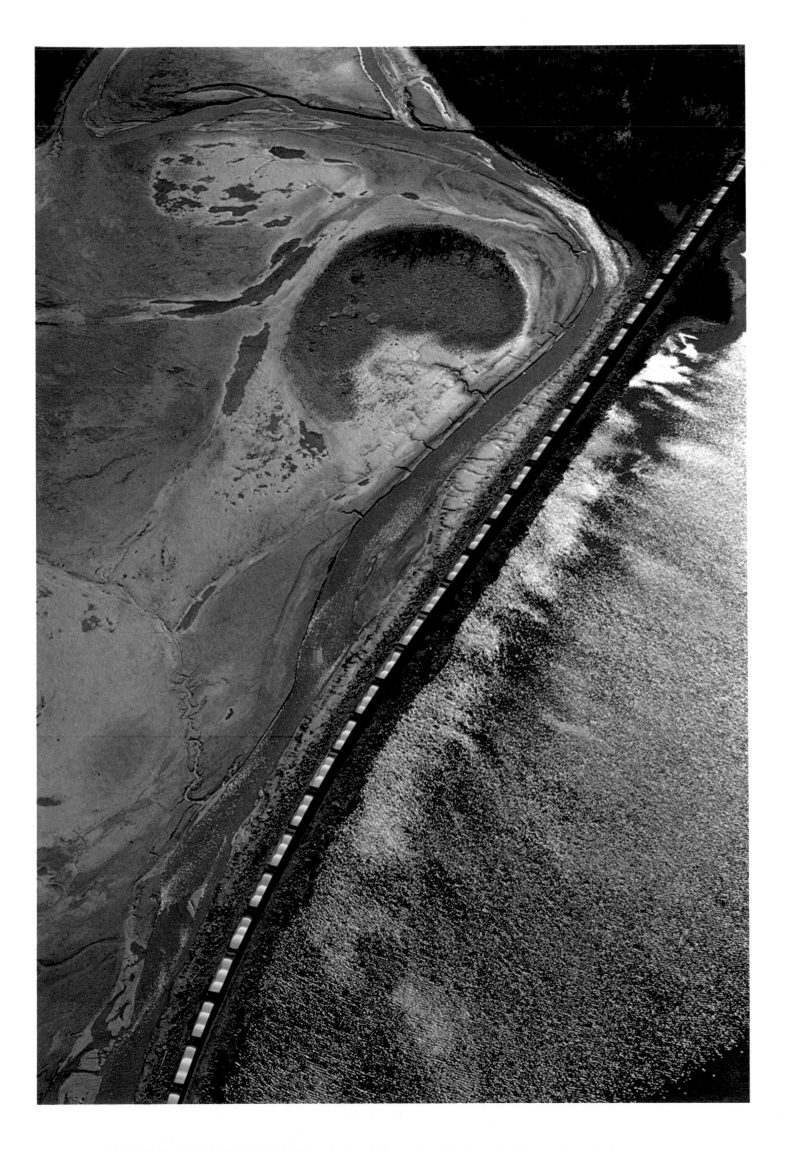

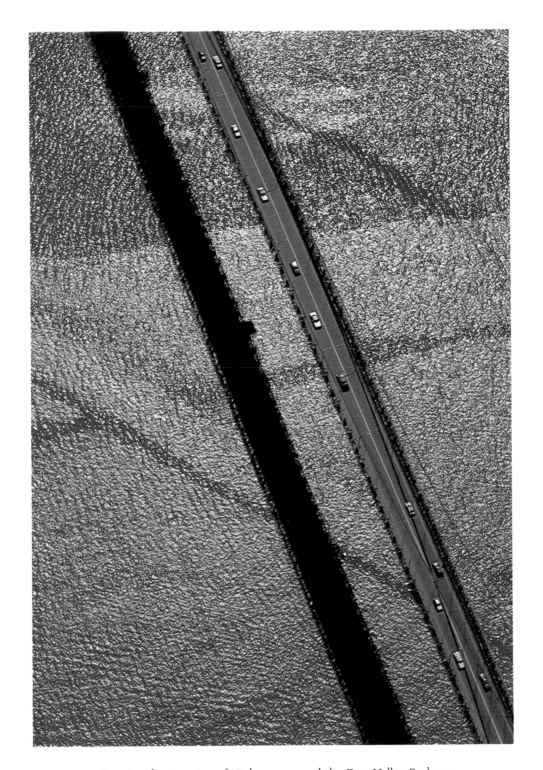

Opposite: The junction of Highway 401 and the Don Valley Parkway forms one of several great concrete and asphalt labyrinths guarding Toronto. With vehicles streaming harmoniously and hypnotically around a mathematically elegant system of lines and curves, the effect from above is rather more like watching a computer-animated model than looking at reality.

A*bove:* The older of two nearly identical suspension spans vaulting the narrows between Halifax and Dartmouth, The Angus L. Macdonald Bridge casts its shadow across the breeze-riffled waters of Halifax harbour.

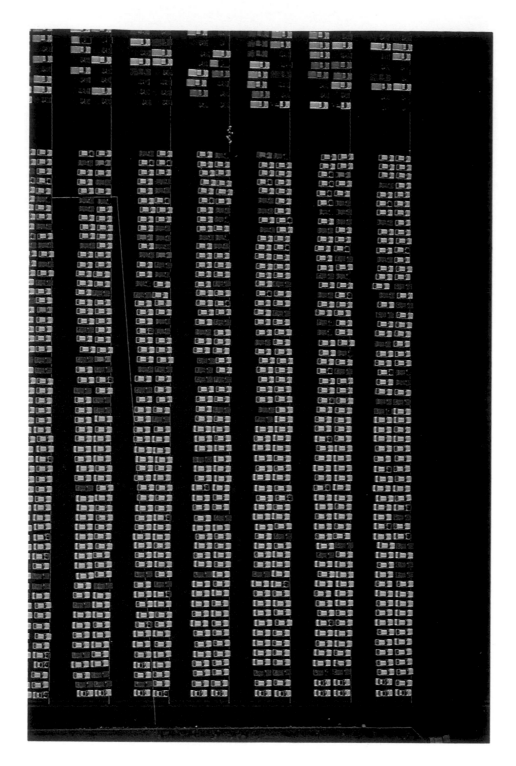

Above: Unbroken ranks of Datsuns at dockside in Richmond, British Columbia, hint at the magnitude of exchange with Japan. Largely through the export of enormous quantities of timber products, coal, grain, and other primary resources, Canada actually enjoys a trade surplus with its second-largest trading partner.

Opposite: The streets of Hinton glisten in the wake of a passing rain shower. On the Hinton Trail from Jasper to the Yukon during the gold rush, the town thrived when the Grand Trunk Pacific Railway reached the Rockies. Next a coal town, subsequently a ghost town after an explosion wrecked its mine, Hinton is today the centre of a pulp and paper industry in the Athabasca Valley.

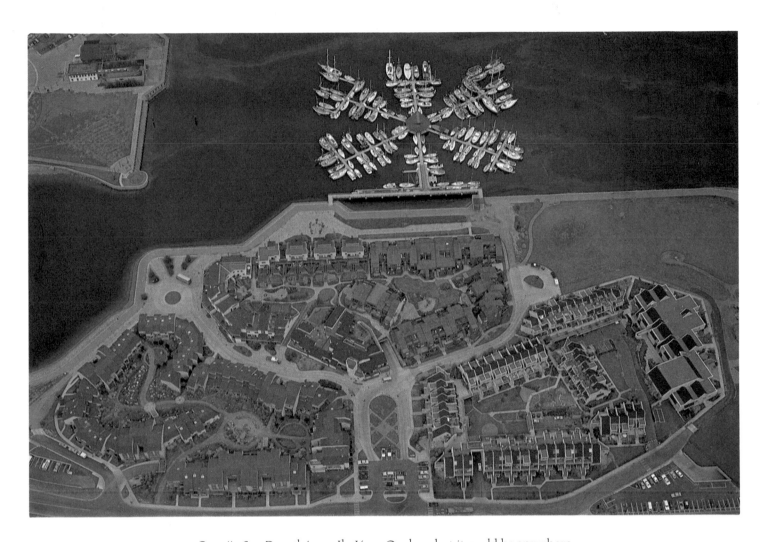

Opposite: Ste.-Dorothée on Ile Jésus, Quebec; but it could be anywhere in suburban central Canada, when summer prompts the erection of a swimming pool in almost every other backyard. The heat and humidity in this part of the country makes a pool a sensible convenience, not just a status symbol.

Above: The result of an urban renewal program, emphatically-roofed row houses at False Creek replace part of the old industrial core of Vancouver. The stellar plan marina elbowing into a tight harbour reflects the fact that space on the busy waterfronts of Vancouver's inlets is severely limited.

Opposite: Centrepiece of the Parliament Buildings, the 302-foot Peace Tower commemorates the dead of four wars. Built of sandstone, its dominance of Ottawa was ensured until the 1960s, when a law that limited new buildings to 150 feet was revoked.

Above: Made of marble from Pennsylvania, Italy, and Quebec, the Legislative Building in Edmonton is a striking landmark, day and night. In the background, Renfrew Park field is lit up for a ball game.

Overleaf: Proud Lunenburg, its neatly painted clapboard buildings filing across the hill between its main and back harbours, has secured a reputation for greatness at sea. Its shipwrights built the *Bluenose* (and its 1963 replica), possibly the greatest sailing ship of the century. While the *Bluenose* enhances the Canadian dime, Lunenburg itself appears on the hundred-dollar bill.

Opposite: Crowned with the world's second-largest octagonal dome after St. Peter's in Rome, St. Joseph's Oratory totally dominates its setting on the northwest slopes of Mount Royal. More than forty years in construction, Canada's largest church had its beginnings in a modest chapel maintained by Brother André, who established a reputation as a miracle worker. The Montreal basilica attracts more than a million pilgrims each year.

Above: The oldest continuously inhabited settlement in North America, Quebec City was strategically sited on the St. Lawrence "where the river narrows" — hence its Indian name, "Kebek." In the palatial style of hotel architecture common at the beginning of the century, the Château Frontenac dominates the colourfully roofed city.

Above: The Royal Bank Building is perhaps the finest of the bank skyscrapers dominating the core of Toronto, and the only one designed by a Canadian firm of architects. Clad in glass coated with a quarter of a million dollars' worth of gold dust, and with a soaring interior lobby between its two towers, it rates as one of the world's most impressive office buildings.

Opposite: Chief landmark of Halifax, the Citadel was the fourth fort built on this hilltop, which commands a view of the entire city. Presenting a low profile from below, the stellar plan defences were never tested in battle. The fort is now a national historic site, and houses three museums.

Opposite: Even if it wasn't the tallest, the CN Tower would still be in a class of its own. Its Y-shaped cross-section elegantly departs from the usual tapering concrete tube structure. The imaginative design provides flat vertical surfaces for outside elevators and allows for views straight down the shaft from the inside of the observation deck.

Above: Brightening minute by minute as dusk deepens, the lights of downtown Vancouver appear as a vibrant starscape below.

Like a starry night, a farm north of Dawson Creek in British Columbia
is dotted with round bales of hay illuminated by the setting sun. A
windbreak of aspen trees casts long shadows across the field.

Edited by José Druker
Designed by David Shaw & Associates Ltd.
Composed by Accurate Typesetting Ltd.
Separated by Flintlock Productions Ltd.
Manufactured in Canada by The Bryant Press Limited